W9-CNK-352

NewYorkCity

New!

New York
N.Y.

HK 59-25-67

APA PUBLICATIONS

Part of the Langenscheidt Publishing Group

L

Welcome!

The Manhattan skyline is one of the most evocative images in the world. It conjures up a sense of excitement, opportunity and change. But New York is much more than the Statue of Liberty and soaring buildings. It is also a rich melange of different peoples with a strongly individualistic frame of mind.

 John Gattuso, Insight's correspondent in New York, embraces both the people and the place, taking readers to all the blockbuster sights while celebrating the city's unique personality en route.

A writer and editor who has worked on many Insight projects, John first got to know New York on outings with his grandmother – on trips to see shows at Radio City Music Hall or to see the dinosaurs at the Museum of Natural History. As he jogged to keep up with the brisk pace she set, he would hear her say, 'There's nothing like New York,' and 'Anything you want, you can find it here,' sentiments that the adult Gattuso wholeheartedly endorses.

In *Insight Pocket Guide: New York* John takes pleasure in sharing his knowledge in a series of carefully crafted itineraries designed specifically for people with only a few days to spend in New York, which, he says, can take a lifetime to understand. Building on Grandma's insights, he has devised three full-day itineraries concentrating on 'must-see' sights, and 14 half-day 'Pick and Mix' itineraries designed for visitors with more time.

C O N T E N T S

Pages 2/3: city image

*Pages 8/9:
soaring architecture*

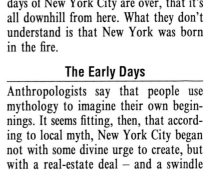

HISTORY & CULTURE

Over 30 million people travel to New York every year. It's the most visited city in the world.

Why do they come? Why do millions of people leave their homes in Duluth, Chicago, Tokyo, Milan or any one of a thousand other places around the globe and come to New York?

Every now and then, the answer comes to me clear as day. It's usually when I'm visiting a museum or drifting through a SoHo gallery. Or when I'm walking down Broadway on the Upper West Side or on Mott Street in Chinatown. And especially when I hear voices on the street, sometimes in three or four different languages, all engaged in conversations within earshot of the others. That's when I know for certain that New York is the most interesting city in the world.

It might sound trite, but New York is a place where anything can happen. It's a city dangerous with possibilities, a rollicking testimony to the creative powers of chaos.

At the heart of it all, of course, is Manhattan, and it's not difficult to see why. Put 1½ million people on a tiny island and they're bound to kick up sparks. Add some of the world's most influential institutions, corporations, artists and thinkers — not to mention

The colonist and the colonized

an immigrant population from every corner of the world — and the sparks ignite a bonfire.

There are people who say that the glory days of New York City are over, that it's all downhill from here. What they don't understand is that New York was born in the fire.

The Early Days

Anthropologists say that people use mythology to imagine their own beginnings. It seems fitting, then, that according to local myth, New York City began not with some divine urge to create, but with a real-estate deal — and a swindle at that. In 1626, a Dutch official by the name of Peter Minuit bought Manhattan Island from the Indians for a box of

View of New York c1730

trinkets worth about $24. Today in the frantic world of downtown Manhattan, $24 buys about half a square inch of office space, or maybe even less.

The Dutch presence in the New York area began in 1609 with the voyage of Henry Hudson. English by birth, Hudson was hired by a Dutch trading company to discover the elusive Northwest Passage to the rich spice markets of India. Hudson didn't have much luck finding the legendary short-cut, but he did stumble on an abundant northern woodland. He was especially interested in the furs worn by local Indians. Furs meant big money in a cold country like the Netherlands. He sent samples back to the company, explaining that the Indians were eager to trade.

Hudson's employers – a thick-headed lot, to be sure – were not impressed. But when word of his discovery leaked out, independent merchants sailed for the New World dreaming of the riches they would bring back in fur. One corporation in particular – the Dutch West India Company – pulled ahead of its competitors, and in 1621 acquired exclusive trading rights to the whole of New Netherland. To seal its claim, the company built trading posts along the coast and inland waterways. One of these settlements, occupied at first by Protestant refugees called Walloons, was established on the southern tip of Manhattan Island. Its name was New Amsterdam.

Life in the Dutch colony was tumultuous. The ground was repeatedly bloodied by Indian massacres, slave uprisings and drunken fights. A despotic, one-legged governor called Peter Stuyvesant was dispatched to straighten out the rowdy settlers, but his iron rule was cut short. After years of coveting the Dutch territory, the English forced Stuyvesant to surrender his post. They renamed the town New York in honor of the King's brother (the Duke of York). The Dutch recaptured the town about 10 years later, but a quick deal at the negotiating table returned it to British hands.

Unfortunately, the English weren't much better at governing the

11

colony than the Dutch, and by the 1760s resentment against King George had reached boiling point. Angered by taxes levied against the colonies, a group of rebels known as the Sons of Liberty spent their time plotting insurrection and taunting British soldiers. In 1770, a spate of nasty skirmishes between protestors and soldiers culminated in the so-called Battle of Golden Hill, leaving one citizen dead and several wounded. The Boston Massacre followed a few weeks later, setting the stage for an all-out revolt. New York was immobilized by the Revolutionary War almost immediately. Despite General George Washington's efforts to defend the city, British troops swept through New York, easily wiping out more than 4,000 militiamen in three bloody engagements. The British settled in for a brutal seven-year occupation during which hundreds of American prisoners were starved to death in makeshift jails.

When Washington returned to New York in 1785 it was to celebrate America's victory and to bid farewell to his officers. If the General had had his way he would have retired to Virginia, never to serve again. But four years later he was back in New York, his hand on a Bible, taking the oath of office. For a single year, New York City was the nation's capital.

Erie Canal and Civil War

In 1825 the Erie Canal opened, connecting the city with the Great Lakes and ripe midwestern markets. Fueled by cheap immigrant labor, New York became an industrial dynamo. Businesses boomed, the arts flourished, and fortunes were quickly built.

For the poor immigrants who did the work — most from Ireland or Germany — it was a time of struggle and frustration. The American Civil War came, and many immigrants answered President Lincoln's call for volunteers. But when a draft law was declared allowing wealthy young men to buy their way out of military service, the poor of New York could simply not contain themselves. For three days, street gangs raged through the city, attacking policemen, burning buildings and lynching people from lampposts. In all, the Draft Riots of 1863 claimed 1,500 lives and cost at least $2 million in damages. The Civil War ended two years later. Within months, Abraham Lincoln's body lay in state at New York City Hall.

The Big Boom

Mass immigration continued after the Civil War and by 1900 New York's population had swelled to more than 3 million people, placing it in the ranks of the world's great cities. With much of the country in shambles, New York easily took the lead in wealth and power. Families such as the Vanderbilts, Morgans, Rockefellers and Astors amassed millions in banking and industry. The famous '400' – the city's upper crust – built enormous uptown mansions, threw lavish parties, and plundered European art.

Downtown, the scene was as wretched as ever. Two thousand immigrants poured into the Ellis Island Immigration Station every day, cramming tenements and sweat shops with more people than they could possibly handle. Families of six or seven often lived in one small room and disease was rife. In 1911, a tragic fire at the Triangle Shirtwaist Company near Washington Square Park claimed 146 lives, finally alerting the public to the appalling conditions under which immigrants were forced to work. In the wake of the tragedy the first fire laws and sprinklers came into being.

Jewish immigrant

As far as politics was concerned, the city was run by Tammany Hall, and Tammany Hall was run by William Marcy Tweed. 'Boss' Tweed and his cronies spent most of their time lining their pockets, milking the city of over $150 million within 10 years. In one spectacular morning, the Tweed Ring raked in a cool $5.5 million on a kickback scheme. Ironically, the contract in question was for the New York City Courthouse (aka the Tweed Courthouse) immediately behind the City Hall. Tweed was eventually exposed by local newspapers, and spent his last desperate days in jail.

From Walker to LaGuardia

World War I came and went with minimal impact on New York City. Business continued to boom, the population grew and the city enjoyed a general sense of well-being. In 1925, James Walker was elected mayor. The wise-cracking, high-living character – a former Tin Pan Alley songwriter – was the perfect embodiment of the Jazz Age, a gambler, lady's man and fashion plate, as loose with money as he was with Prohibition. When he decided to raise his own salary

Fiorello LaGuardia

by $10,000, critics attacked his extravagance. The Mayor's reply was typical Jimmy Walker: 'Think what it would cost if I worked full-time.'

When the stock market crashed in 1929, Walker's reign of good feelings came tumbling down with it. The Great Depression hit New York hard, and Walker was no match for the job that lay ahead. Word of corruption had reached the papers, and Walker was dragged into court. He resigned his office in 1932 under a gathering cloud of scandal.

About a year later, a new mayor moved into City Hall. He was a small, rather plump man with none of Walker's finesse. But for a city ravaged by the Depression, he was the closest thing to a savior anyone could hope for. Fiorello LaGuardia was elected in 1933 and immediately got on board Franklin Roosevelt's New Deal, launching massive relief and construction programs in an effort to revive the economy. His administration swung into action, building bridges, parks, houses, even finding work for artists and writers. At the same time, private investors poured money into large-scale construction. The Chrysler Building, the Empire State Building and the massive Rockefeller Center, for example, were all built in the early 1930s.

Rockefeller Center

In 1941, the US entered World War II, and New York found itself swept into the war effort. Japanese families were rounded up and sent to Ellis Island, blackouts were ordered and even the torch on the Statue of Liberty was turned off. In the basement of a Columbia University physics laboratory, scientists were experimenting with atomic fission, laying down crucial groundwork for the development of the atomic bomb, better known by its code name, the Manhattan Project.

Brink of Disaster

With the United Nations meeting in the city in 1946, New York was flush with a sense of possibilities. World peace, a healthy economy, the riches of technology – they all seemed within reach. But as in many of America's other northeastern cities, the post-war years brought an unexpected turn for the worse. The middle class began moving out to other boroughs as well as the suburbs, corporations relocated, and poor blacks and Hispanics flooded the city. With its tax base weakened and public services at an all-time high, the city was in a financial stranglehold. The situation was exacerbated by high-level corruption, with organized crime infiltrating government. By 1975, New York was teetering dangerously on the edge of bankruptcy.

In 1976, Edward Koch was elected mayor and an effort was launched to buoy the city budget with massive borrowing. A resurgence of corporate development injected new capital into the economy, and the city gradually got back on its feet.

In 1989, David Dinkins became the city's first African-American mayor; in 1993, he lost the mayoral election to Rudolph Giuliani, a former public prosecutor. As usual, the city found itself in the throes of transition. But then, that's what makes New York what it is and it is why people like it. Nothing stays the same here, and that's the way it should be.

There are a few things you can always count on, though: world-class museums and art galleries, a wild array of different food and shopping, stunning architecture, great entertainment, people from every corner of the planet, earth-shattering business deals, outrageous street life and a frenzied non-stop rhythm. In the end, this is a city about living and change, excitement and struggle, joy and ambition. Anything can happen in New York, good or bad. There are exciting possibilities at every turn. Realities no one suspected. That's what makes it such an interesting place to live in and visit. As soon as you understand New York, your understanding is obsolete.

Manhattan skyline

Historical Highlights

1000: Algonquin Indian tribes use Manhattan for summer hunting and fishing.

1524: Giovanni da Verrazano, sailing for Francis I of France, sights Manhattan but doesn't land.

1609: Henry Hudson sails into New York Harbor and up the Hudson River.

1624: The Dutch West India Company establishes a settlement on the southern tip of Manhattan at the current site of Battery Park.

1626: Dutch Governor Peter Minuit 'buys' Manhattan from local Indians for about 60 guilders, roughly $24.

1643: Conflict with local Algonquin tribes leaves about 80 Indians dead at the Pavonia Massacre.

1647: Peter Stuyvesant is named director general of New Netherland.

1653: Stuyvesant builds a fence along Wall Street with the aim of protecting New Amsterdam from British incursion.

1664: Stuyvesant surrenders New Amsterdam to the British without firing a shot. The English rename it New York, after King Charles II's brother, James, Duke of York.

1673: The Dutch recapture New York and rename it New Orange, again without a fight.

1674: New York is returned to the British as a result of the Treaty of Westminster, ending Dutch-British hostilities.

1689: New York merchant, James Leisler, stages a revolt against British rule and as a result is hanged for treason.

1712: Black slaves set fire to a home on Maiden Lane, hoping to incite an insurrection. Nine whites are killed. Six of the slaves commit suicide; 21 others hanged.

1735: Newspaper publisher John Peter Zenger is tried for slandering the British crown. He is acquitted, establishing the precedent for freedom of the press.

1765: Unfair taxes, including the Sugar, Colonial Currency and Stamp Acts, are levied against the colonists.

1770: Skirmishes between the Sons of Liberty and British soldiers culminate in the Battle of Golden Hill.

1776: The Revolutionary War begins. Washington loses New York to General William Howe.

1789: George Washington is inaugurated at the site of Federal Hall, Wall Street. New York serves as the federal capital until 1790.

1792: A rudimentary form of the New York Stock Exchange is organized to help boost the economy.

1825: Erie Canal opens, giving New York industry and trade immediate access to midwestern markets.

1830: Irish and German immigrants begin arriving in great numbers. Immigration continues well into the 1850s and beyond.

1835: Lower Manhattan is ravaged by the Great Fire.

1857: William Marcy 'Boss' Tweed, elected to the county board of supervisors, launches a 14-year career of notorious corruption.

1858: Work begins on Central Park.

1861: The American Civil War is declared.

1863: Draft Riots tear the city apart for three days. Approximately 1,500 people are killed.

1865: Immigration continues unabated. Italians, East European Jews and Chinese arrive in unprecedented numbers well into the 1920s.

1871: Boss Tweed is arrested; dies in jail.

1877: The Museum of Natural History opens.

1880: Metropolitan Museum of Art opens.

1883: The Brooklyn Bridge opens.

1886: The Statute of Liberty is unveiled on Liberty Island.

Rockefeller Center detail

1888: The Great Blizzard paralyzes the city.

1891: Carnegie Hall opens. Tchaikovsky conducts during opening ceremonies.

1892: Ellis Island Immigration Station opens.

1898: New York's five boroughs are united under one single municipal government.

1911: Triangle fire alerts public to the appalling work and living conditions of poor immigrants.

1929: Stock Market crashes. Onset of the Great Depression.

1931: The Empire State Building opens.

1932: Scandal-ridden Mayor James Walker resigns.

1933: Fiorello LaGuardia is elected mayor.

1941: The United States enters World War II.

1952: United Nations moves to its present site.

1959: Construction work begins on Lincoln Center.

1966: Work begins on the World Trade Center.

1975: New York City faces bankruptcy, saved by federal loans.

1978: Edward Koch is elected mayor.

1982: IBM Building opens, followed by the AT&T Building in 1983, affirming resurgence of corporate development

1986: Battery Park City opens. Statue of Liberty is restored for the centennial celebration.

1990: David Dinkins takes over mayor's office.

1994: Former prosecutor Rudolph W. Giuliani becomes the city's first Republican mayor since John Lindsay in the 1960s.

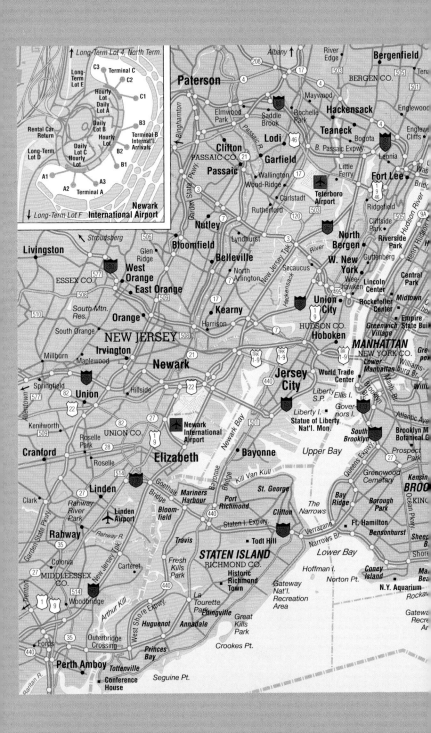

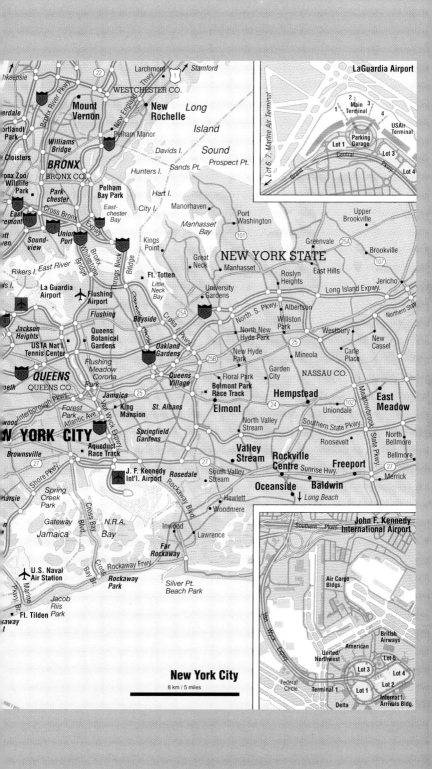

LaGuardia Airport

Lot 6, 7, Marine Air Terminal

Main Terminal
1 2 3 4
USAir Terminal

Parking Garage

Lot 1
Lot 2
Central
Lot 3
Grand
Lot 4

Larchmont   *Stamford*
(22)
WESTCHESTER CO.
Mount Vernon
New Rochelle
Long Island
New England Thwy.
Pelham Manor
Williams Bridge
Davids I.   *Sound*
Cloisters
Hunters I.   *Sands Pt.*   Prospect Pt.
Bronx River Pkwy.
BRONX
BRONX CO.
Pelham Bay Park
Park-chester
Eastchester Bay
City I.
Manorhaven   Port Washington
Upper Brookville
Cross Bronx
Soundview
Union Port
Rikers I.   *East River*
Hart I.
Manhasset Bay
(101)
Greenvale (25A)   Brookville
(107)
Bronx Zoo/Wildlife Park
Kings Point
Great Neck
NEW YORK STATE
Manhasset
Roslyn Heights
East Hills   Jericho
La Guardia Airport
Throgs Neck Bridge
Bronx Whitestone Bridge
Ft. Totten
Little Neck Bay
University Gardens
Long Island Expwy.
Flushing Airport
North. S. Pkwy.   Albertson
Northern State
Flushing
Bayside
Willston Park
Westbury   New Cassel
Jackson Heights
Cross Pkwy.
(25A)
North New Hyde Park
(25)
USTA Nat'l Tennis Center
Queens Botanical Gardens
Oakland Gardens
New Hyde Park
Carle Place
Mineola
Flushing Meadow Corona Park
(25B)
Garden City
NASSAU CO.
QUEENS
QUEENS CO.
Queens Village
Floral Park
Meadowbrook State Pkwy.
Jamaica
(25)
St. Albans
Belmont Park Race Track
Hempstead
East Meadow
Forest Park
King Mansion
(24)
Elmont
Uniondale
(102)
Interborough Pkwy.
Atlantic Ave.
North Valley Stream
Southern State Pkwy.
N YORK CITY
Van Wyck Expwy.
Springfield Gardens
Roosevelt
North Bellmore
Brownsville
Aqueduct Race Track
(27)
Valley Stream
Rockville Centre
Sunrise Hwy.
Freeport
Bellmore
Shore Pkwy.
Rosedale
South Valley Stream
Oceanside
Baldwin
Merrick
(27)
Spring Creek Park
J. F. Kennedy Int'l. Airport
Rockaway Blvd.
Hewlett   ↓ *Long Beach*
marsie
Gateway   N.R.A.
Woodmere
Cross Bay Blvd.
Jamaica   Bay
Inwood
Lawrence
n
U.S. Naval Air Station
Rockaway Frwy.
Far Rockaway
Marine
Cross Bay Br.
Rockaway Park
Silver Pt. Beach Park
Pkwy.
Jacob Riis Park
Ft. Tilden Park
away

John F. Kennedy International Airport
Southern   Pkwy.
Air Cargo Bldgs.
Van Wyck Expwy.
British Airways
United/Northwest
American
Lot 5
Federal Circle
Lot 3
Lot 4
Terminal 1
Lot 1
Lot 2
Delta
Internat'l. Arrivals Bldg.

New York City
8 km / 5 miles

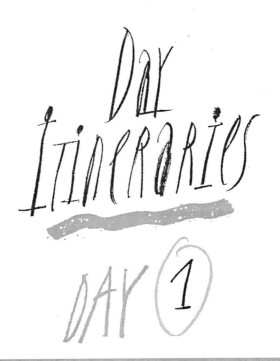

Day Itineraries

DAY 1

Breakfast at the Plaza, followed by the Empire State Building and Fifth Avenue. Lunch on West 57th Street, and later a sunset cruise around Manhattan and dinner at Rockefeller Center.

Your first day is designed to acquaint you with Manhattan by looking at it from three very different points of view. The first is from the sky, 1,000 ft (304 meters) above the city. The second is from the bustling heart of midtown. And the third is from a ship cruising around the island.

Kick off your first day in high style. Treat yourself to breakfast at the **Plaza Hotel**. It will set you back a few dollars, but the Plaza's old-world elegance is worth every penny. And so is the location, right on Fifth Avenue across from Central Park. Ask for the **Edwardian Room**, a lavish oak-paneled salon with a gorgeous view of the park, not to mention the beautiful clientele. In days past, people like Mark Twain, Frank Lloyd Wright and Eleanor Roosevelt made the Plaza their home away from home. If you hang around long enough you're likely to see more than one celebrity striding down the stairway to a waiting limousine.

After breakfast, hop into a cab outside the lobby and ask the driver to take you down to the **Empire State Building**, which rises like a rocket from the corner of Fifth

View from the top

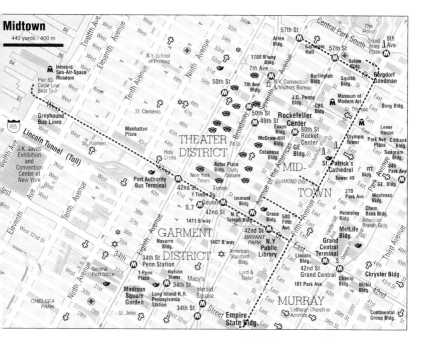

Avenue and 34th Street. When it was completed in 1931, this was
the highest building in the world. Today, it ranks third behind the
Sears Tower in Chicago and the World Trade Center in the financial district. But when it comes to the view it can't be beat: on a
clear day you can see as far as 80 miles (128km). Take the elevator to the 86th-floor observation deck at the concourse level; a second elevator goes from here up to the tiny lookout on the 102nd
floor, which is just about where Fay Wray had her fateful rendezvous with a 50-ft (15-meter) ape by the name of King Kong.

Back on street level, start your walk north (ie uptown) on **Fifth
Avenue**. The legendary playground of New York's oldest and wealth-
iest families, Fifth is actually a bit tedious in this part of midtown.
The elegant townhouses once owned by the Astors and the Vanderbilts have since been replaced by discount shops and the permanent 'going-out-of-business' signs they use
to lure customers.

Standing guard

The one major exception, of courses, is the
New York Public Library, located right at
the corner of 42nd Street. Built in 1911, this
grand Beaux Arts monument now houses
one of the finest research facilities in the
world. An unlikely mix of office workers,
layabouts and footsore tourists can usually
be found lounging on the stairway under the
gaze of 'Patience' and 'Fortitude,' the two
marble lions reclining on the top step.

Turn left on **West 44th Street** for a look
at the handsome neo-Georgian facade of
the **Harvard Club**, the fanciful windows of

21

Christmas at Rockefeller Center

the **New York Yacht Club**, and the **Algonquin Hotel**, where the city's literary elite gathered at the famous Round Table; across the street the **Royalton Hotel**'s '44' restaurant is populated with more contemporary literary lunchers.

Farther up on Fifth, a left turn at West 47th Street takes you into the **Diamond District**, where close to $500 million in gems is traded every day, most of it by Hasidic Jews who you'll see wearing black suits, wide-brimmed hats, long beards and side locks. Book-lovers should make a point of stopping at the **Gotham Book Mart** (41 W. 47th St), a favorite browsing place of writers such as Eugene O'Neill, Tennessee Williams and Saul Bellow. A block up Fifth, between 48th and 49th streets, art lovers can browse the collection of 19th-century European art at the second-floor **Dahesh Museum** (601 Fifth Avenue, open Tuesday through Saturday from 11am to 4pm).

At **49th Street**, Fifth Avenue finally begins to live up to its legend, thanks to **Rockefeller Center**, the world's largest privately owned business and entertainment complex and an absolute triumph of Art Deco architecture. The **Channel Gardens** – so named because they separate La Maison Française on the left and the British Building on the right – draw visitors into the center of the plaza, dominated by the soaring mass of the **GE Building** (30 Rockefeller Plaza). The GE Building is fronted by a sunken courtyard used as an outdoor restaurant in summer and an ice-skating rink in winter. The 18-ft (5-meter) gilded statue of Prometheus is the work of Paul Manship.

Lee Lawrie's striking stone relief, *Genius*, looms over the entrance; inside, the main lobby features two murals by Jose Maria Sert, *American Progress* and *Time*. Originally Diego Rivera was commissioned for the paintings, but when he refused to change a panel with Lenin on it, the Rockefellers fired him. Before leaving, stop at the lobby information desk to find out about taking one of the **NBC Studio** tours offered regularly throughout the day (call 664-7174 for details).

St Patrick's Cathedral

A massive bronze sculpture of Atlas, also by Lee Lawrie, stands in front of the International Building between 50th and 51st streets, although it's dwarfed by **St Patrick's Cathedral**, on the other side of Fifth Avenue. Opened in 1879, St. Patrick's is now one of midtown's most formidable landmarks; its ornate Gothic facade counterpoints against the angular lines and smooth surfaces of the skyscrapers around it. Take some time for a close look at the cathedral's magnificent interior. The bronze doors and stained-glass windows are particularly impressive.

Beyond St Pat's, Fifth Avenue devotes itself to more worldly concerns – money and lots of it. **Saks Fifth Avenue**, one of the city's finest department stores, is across the street from Rockefeller Center. The super-rich (and those who like to pretend) can be seen bouncing between Cartier, Fortunoff, Bijan and Gucci near 54th Street, just to name a few of the high-class boutiques that give the area its panache. The ornate façade of **St Thomas' Church** overlooks it all from 53rd Street – and if you have any interest in religious art, be sure to stop in to admire its magnificent sanctuary, or perhaps one of the organ recitals or choir rehearsals sometimes open to the public. Just beyond the stately brownstone Fifth Avenue Presbyterian Church, you'll find **Henri Bendel** (712 Fifth Avenue), clothier of choice for the ultra-chic. Farther up, at 56th Street, **Steuben Glass** is renowned for its beautiful displays of museum-quality crystal.

Fifth Avenue's glitz is epitomized by **Trump Tower**, between 56th and 57th streets. The 68-story complex includes restaurants, stores and pricey condominium apartments. The shops are beyond the budgets of mere mortals, too, but the window shopping is free. Get an eyeful of the exquisite American Indian jewelry at **Saity Jewelry**. The display window alone rivals museum collections.

By the time you're finished exploring Trump Tower, you will probably be thinking about lunch. Take one of two options. If Trump suits your style, try the atrium cafe next to the waterfall; otherwise, exit back on to Fifth Avenue and turn right toward 57th Street. You are now headed for one of the city's densest concentrations of shops and art galleries.

East 57th kicks off with **Tiffany and Co.**, world-famous designers of glassware and jewelry, and moves around the corner to **Louis Vuitton**, **Hermes** and **Chanel**, all on the block between Fifth and Madison avenues.

A show of patriotism, Trump Tower

The city doesn't sleep

Back on the northeast corner of Fifth, the **Warner Bros. Studio Store** is a mecca of mass-merchandizing in action; stop in and take a look before crossing Fifth Avenue to **West 57th**. Pass up the jewels glittering in the windows of **Van Cleef & Arpel**, and instead, duck into the **Sharper Image** (4 W. 57th St), stacked with grown-up toys such as a two-man hovercraft. Be sure to save plenty of time for **Rizzoli Bookstore** (31 W. 57th St), a beautiful wood-paneled mansion with an international selection of literature and music.

Between Fifth and Sixth avenues (as well as east of Fifth), 57th Street boasts one of the city's densest collections of prestigious art galleries, including **The Marlborough Gallery** (40 W. 57th St), **Gallery 84** and **George Adams** (both at 50 W. 57th St). A walk farther west will also bring you to **Carnegie Hall**, at the corner of Seventh Avenue. The concert hall's reputation is perhaps more impressive than its appearance. Industrialist Andrew Carnegie managed to persuade Tchaikovsky to conduct during the grand opening in 1891, and the stage has attracted the world's finest performers ever since.

The Hard Rock Cafe

If you haven't eaten already, now is the time to do it. The **Hard Rock Cafe**, about half a block away (look for the rear end of a Cadillac hanging over the door) is known more for its kitsch than its kitchen, but the burgers and sandwiches aren't bad. Movie buffs may enjoy **Planet Hollywood** (140 W. 57th St), a glitzy movie-theme eatery back toward Sixth Avenue. Another popular spot is the **Motown Cafe** (104 W. 57th). Or try the **Russian Tea Room** (150 W. 57th St), founded by members of the Russian Corps de Ballet, which may have reopened following renovations. More movie deals were cut over the original restaurant's vodka and caviar than anywhere else in the city.

After lunch take another taxi, this time to the **Circle Line** at

Pier 83, on the Hudson River (West Side Highway at 42nd Street). These three-hour minicruises generally depart between 9.30am and 4.30pm; later on weekends and in summer. Plan on making the 2.30 or 3.30pm departure (for prices and schedules, call 563-3200), which should leave time to return to your hotel before dinner.

Plan on eating at about 8 or 8.30pm, but remember that reservations are crucial if you want to avoid a long wait. For romantic atmosphere and a wonderful view, you can't beat the **Rainbow Room**, perched on the 65th floor of 30 Rockefeller Center. It is, however, both formal and extremely expensive (jacket and tie required here and at the smaller **Rainbow and Stars** cabaret) and might be best saved for a big splurge, if you can afford it. Instead, head for the **Sea Grill** or, less pricey, the **American Festival Cafe**, both in the lower plaza.

Uptown

Breakfast on the Upper East Side. Museum-hopping on Fifth and Madison avenues; and a stroll in Central Park. Dinner on the Upper West Side, followed by a horse-drawn carriage ride.

Uptown refers to the area between 59th and 86th streets. The heart of this part of the city is **Central Park**, a peaceful 843-acre (340-ha) oasis of lakes and meadows that, for many New Yorkers, is the spiritual calm at the eye of the storm.

The neighborhoods on either side of Central Park are like twin brothers separated at birth – similar in appearance but different in attitude. On the **Upper East Side**, wealth prevails; the home of the comfortable rich and people who have quite clearly 'arrived.' The **Upper West Side**, on the other hand, is still about struggle. In some cases that literally means a struggle for survival, in others a struggle for a second BMW. And although there are wealthy sections on the West Side, like the magnificent apartments on **Central Park West**, there are also patches of destitution. Somewhere in the middle, the 'urban gentry' – commonly known as yuppies – try to work their way out of the middle class.

The uptown tour starts with a hearty breakfast at **Sarabeth's Kitchen** (1295 Madison Avenue near East 93rd Street) on the ground floor of the

Urban idyll

The Guggenheim Museum

Hotel Wales, an inviting cafe where the menu includes delicious home-made jam. You'll be doing a lot of walking, so be sure to eat your fill. In fact, it's not a bad idea to get a couple of muffins to go, just in case you want a few nibbles along the way.

After breakfast, walk up to 95th Street and turn left toward Fifth Avenue. This is nearly the top of **Museum Mile**, a 35-block stretch of Fifth Avenue bordering Central Park which is home to some of the city's most prestigious museums. If you turn left on Fifth, heading downtown, you immediately come to the International Center of Photography (94th St), the Jewish Museum (92nd St), the Cooper-Hewitt National Design Museum (2 E. 91st St) and the National Academy of Design (89th St), all well worth exploring. For now, at least, pass them up for something a bit more daring – the **Solomon R. Guggenheim Museum**.

Located on 1071 Fifth Avenue at the corner of 88th Street, the Guggenheim's white funnel-shaped structure has been the source of debate ever since it opened in 1959. Some people say that Frank Lloyd Wright's design, some 16 years in the making, is an architectural masterpiece. Others think it's more akin to a parking garage than an art gallery and definitely out of place next to the handsome townhouses that give the Upper East Side its special charm.

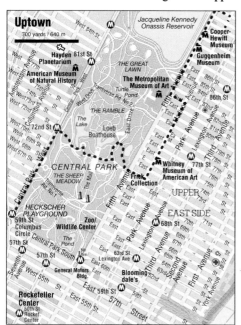

Whatever your opinion, take the elevator to the top floor and slowly make your way down the spiral ramp. Although exhibitions change frequently, they are likely to include works by Renoir, Chagall, Degas, van Gogh, Toulouse-Lautrec, Gauguin, Kandinsky, Klee and Picasso. All in all, not a bad crowd. The Guggenheim opens at 10am Friday to Wednesday; pay what you wish on Friday nights from 6pm to 8pm; closed on Thursday. Regular admission is $10, $7 for students and seniors.

From the Guggenheim, continue down Fifth Avenue to 82nd Street and stop at the **Metropolitan Museum of Art** (Tuesday to Thursday and Sunday 9.30am–5.15pm, Friday and Saturday 9.30am–8.45pm; suggested admission is $8; $4 for students and seniors), a sprawling Gothic behemoth built in stages beginning in 1874 and now the largest art museum in the United States. If you go to only one museum in New York City, this should be it. Not a single museum at all, but over a dozen distinct collections housed in a maze of galleries, gardens and period rooms, the Met's 'must sees' include the American Wing, which contains one of the best collections of American art in the world; a series of intriguing new 19-century European Paintings and Sculpture galleries; and the magnificent Egyptian Collection's reconstructed Temple of Dendur. African, Native American and Pacific Island art can be admired in the Michael C. Rockefeller wing, and the Islamic, Greco-Roman, and Far Eastern art collections here are truly spectacular. You can pick up handy maps and listings of special exhibits and upcoming events from the information booth in the Great Hall, located just inside the Metropolitan's Fifth Avenue entrance.

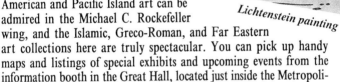

Lichtenstein painting

Leaving the Met behind, turn at 82nd Street and walk one block east to Madison Avenue. The heart of the Upper East Side's high-powered consumer culture, Madison boasts the city's glossiest array of boutiques and galleries. A stand-out exception along the way is the **Whitney Museum of American Art** (945 Madison Ave) at 75th Street (open 11am–6pm Wednesday and Friday to Sunday, 1–8pm on Thursday; admission $8 ($7 for students and senior citizens; free Thursday 6–8pm). Marcel Breuer's cantilevered structure is a work of art in its own right, and it stands with the

The Metropolitan Museum, Rockefeller Primitive Art Collection

Summer in Central Park

Guggenheim as one of the Upper East Side's boldest architectural statements.

Founded in 1930 by Gertrude Vanderbilt Whitney, whose taste ran to American realists like Edward Hopper, the Whitney since then has made a policy of acquiring pieces that represent the full range of 20th-century American art, including the works of Georgia O'Keefe, Willem de Kooning and Jasper Johns. Be sure to stop in at the **Store Next Door**, a nifty little gift shop stocked with an eclectic collection of crafts and jewelry.

In fact, from the Whitney down to 62nd Street, Madison Avenue is a veritable orgy of consumption, with the names above the stores reading like a roster of the international fashion elite: from Yves Saint Laurent and Emanuel Ungaro to Giorgio Armani and Ralph Lauren. You will also find several chic cafes here and on adjoining side streets, but for an authentic (and cheaper) New York culinary experience, stop off for lunch at the **3 Guys Coffee Shop**, across from the Whitney, or the Madison Avenue Cafe, on the corner of 74th Street. Providing it's the right time of year, you might prefer to pick up a sandwich and beverage to go, then walk back to Fifth Avenue and make your way to **Central Park** at 72nd Street for a picnic.

You can pick up fancier provisions at **E.A.T**, at 1064 Madison and 80th Street, or if you don't mind the extra hike, head for **Grace's Marketplace** (1237 Third Avenue, near 72nd St), a gourmet shop crammed with take-out treats. (You may want to take a cab back.)

If you take the first path on your right from the park's 72nd Street entrance, you'll come to the pond-like **Conservatory Water**. Find a bench and watch the model boat enthusiasts while you eat. A little further in, the 18-acre (7.3-ha) **Lake** offers spectacular views of the surrounding skyline. If you're feeling energetic, you can rent a rowboat at the Loeb Boathouse; if you're thirsty, stop for a drink at the **Boathouse Cafe** (72nd St and East Park Drive), which stays open from May through October. Otherwise, follow the path south around the Lake to **Bethesda Terrace**, with its ornate, angel-crowned fountain that was sculpted by Emma Stebbins in 1870. The terrace overlooks the lake, and is particularly lively on warm-weather Saturdays. If you need help finding your way, don't be afraid to ask. New Yorkers positively love to give directions to strangers.

Despite the park's reputation for crime, you shouldn't have any problems during the day. All the same, it's important to be careful. Avoid remote or heavily wooded areas and, if possible, travel with at least one other person. Never go into the park at night unless you're attending a concert or other performance, and even then you should enter and leave with a crowd of other people.

Roller-bladers in the park

Exit Central Park on the west side at 72nd Street, near **Strawberry Fields**, a quiet knoll dedicated to the memory of John Lennon who lived in the **Dakota Building** across the street. When the Dakota was built in 1884, New Yorkers joked that it was so far outside the city, it might as well be in the Dakota Territory. The rest of the city soon caught up with it, however, and the Dakota became the standard against which the other buildings on the West Side are measured.

To the left of the Dakota, between 71st and 72nd streets, stands the **Majestic Apartments**, and two blocks up, between 74th and 75th streets, the equally splendid **San Remo Apartments**.

At this point, you're probably near exhaustion so make a beeline for your hotel and take a rest before returning to the Upper West Side for dinner.

There are so many good restaurants here it's almost absurd to make recommendations. Nonetheless, if you don't mind spending big bucks, you can't possibly go wrong at **Cafe des Artistes** (1 W. 67th St), an exquisite hideaway on the ground floor of the Hotel des Artistes. Alternatively walk over to the **Tavern on the Green**, just inside Central Park at West 67th Street. The patio is at its best on warm autumn evenings, the food is more reasonably priced than you might expect, and the surrounding scenery makes dining here a quintessential New York experience.

After dinner, follow Central Park West down to Columbus Circle and hire one of the **horse-drawn carriages**, which line up along Central Park South, for a leisurely evening ride along Central Park West. It isn's exactly cheap: expect to pay about $34 for the first 30 minutes, and around $10 for another 15, but hey, you only live once.

One option for dinner
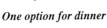

Downtown

440 yards / 400 m

LOWER WEST SIDE

WEST VILLAGE

VILLAGE

LITTLE ITALY

BOWERY

LOWER EAST

SOHO

CHINA-TOWN

TRIBECA

CIVIC CENTER

BATTERY PARK CITY (U.C)

LOWER MANHATTAN

FINANCIAL DISTRICT

SOUTH PARK

BATTERY PARK

River

Hudson River

East River

Holland Tunnel (Toll)

Brooklyn Bridge

Elevated Highway

Brooklyn Queens Exp

DAY ③

Downtown

Breakfast at the Marriott World Trade Center Hotel. A stroll along the Battery Park City esplanade, then a trip to the Statue of Liberty. Lunch and shopping at South Street Seaport. Dinner in Little Italy and late-night jazz in Greenwich Village.

Downtown starts at 14th Street and stretches south to Battery Park. This is the oldest part of Manhattan and undoubtedly the quirkiest. It's also the most confusing – a sort of neighborhood hodgepodge jigsawed together without any real organizing theme. It is as if someone gave the city a good shake and all the loose pieces fell to the bottom. The streets are crooked, the subways tangled, and there are no natural boundaries between one neighborhood and another. To make it even more eclectic, the place is rife with oddball couplings – Jews and Puerto Ricans on the Lower East Side, Italians and Chinese near City Hall, industry and art in SoHo, and a gleaming skyline just around the corner from run-down tenements.

The World Trade Center

In part, at least, it's the incongruities that give downtown its creative spark. If you're looking for innovation, for bold new ideas – whether in art, politics, business or culture – downtown is the place to go. It may the oldest part of the city, but it's still an urban frontier.

The downtown tour starts with breakfast at the **Greenhouse Café** at the Marriott Hotel (3 World Trade Center). From here make a separate trip to the Twin Towers' 107th-floor **Observatory**. This

is where tight-rope walker Philipe Petit made his famous walk between the twin towers. Other daredevils have parachuted off the building and climbed up the side – and were promptly arrested by the New York Police Department. The Observation Deck opens

Battery Park City Esplanade

for conventional visits at 9.30am and costs $10 for adults, $5 for children.

When you come down from the clouds, take in a more earthly spectacle along the riverfront in Battery Park City. From the Observation Deck, take the elevator down to the concourse level and then follow signs to the World Financial Center's North Bridge. Cross over the glass-enclosed walkway and head straight into the **Winter Garden**, a stunning glass atrium with a bevy of high-class shops, a cascading marble stairway and, believe it or not, a small grove of palm trees. Spend some time browsing at Rizzoli Bookshop (3 World Financial Center), have a cup of espresso at one of the cafes, then exit through the Courtyard to the **Esplanade**, which runs for about a mile along the Hudson River toward Battery Park. Along the way you'll come to the new **Museum of Jewish Heritage**, where exhibitions focus on 20th-century Jewish history and the Holocaust (18 First Place; closed Friday afternoons and Saturday, admission $7).

At the southern tip of Manhattan, **Battery Park** is named for the battery of cannons that once stood here; today, it's a pleasant oasis dotted with benches and war memorials, including an old military fortress called **Castle Clinton** where you can buy tickets for the Statue of Liberty and Ellis Island ferry. Boats depart from the nearby South Ferry landing every 30–45 minutes; the return fare is $7 for adults, $3 for children (under 18).

The **Statue of Liberty** was designed by Frederic Auguste Bartholdi and was given to the United States by the French government as a symbol of mutual respect and friendship. Since it was dedicated in 1886, it has not only become one of the most widely recognized American symbols but a welcoming beacon to millions of the country's immigrants, whose first glimpse of the United States was New York Harbor.

Most people who visit the Statue of Liberty want to climb to the top, and as long as you're reasonably fit and don't mind waiting in line (sometimes as much as two hours or more), there's no reason why you shouldn't. This is one of the world's greatest tourist attractions, after all, and since you just schlepped

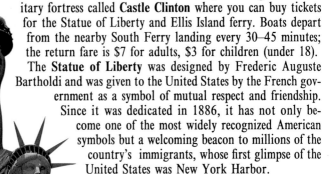

Ms Liberty

all the way out here you might as well get your money's worth. If your idea of vigorous exercise is walking the dog, however, you might want to give it a second thought. Keep in mind that the only way up is a narrow spiral staircase 12 stories high, which means you'll not only be exhausted when you get to the top, but dizzier than a dervish. There's no air conditioning either, which is no big deal on a cool day but absolute hell on a hot one, especially when there are hundreds of people pressed inside. Needless too say, people with heart problems or other medical conditions are discouraged from making the climb.

There's a small immigration museum at the statue's base, but the bigger picture is presented at **Ellis Island**, where exhibits delve into the stories of immigrants who passed through during the 32 years – between 1898 and 1924 – it served as the main gateway to the United States. If you're planning to visit, be sure to take a morning ferry, otherwise you won't have enough time to see it all. Allow for at least an hour on each island, not including ferry time (approximately half an hour each way).

For a quicker glimpse of Lady Liberty, hop on board the Staten Island Ferry, which departs from the terminal at the east end of Battery Park, at Whitehall Street. The roundtrip to Staten Island and back (expect about five minutes turnaround time) also offers spectacular free views of Lower Manhattan.

On your return, walk straight through Battery Park to State Street. Turn right and continue north along Water Street past Chase Manhattan Bank and the **Vietnam Veterans Memorial**, as far as Fulton. Here, turn right and walk directly into the South Street **Seaport Museum.**

Winter Garden in summer

The Seaport is one place where even New Yorkers feel like tourists. Don't let the name fool you. It's not really a museum so much as an enclave of historic buildings converted into a trendy marketplace à la Boston's Quincy Market or London's Covent Garden. After years of neglect, the area was rediscovered by commercial developers, and before New Yorkers knew what hit them, a phenomenon was born. The 19th-century buildings that once housed shipping firms and sailmakers are now occupied by boutiques, cafes and restaurants. About the only thing that hasn't changed is the old **Fulton Fish Market**. It's still the city's busiest fish wholesaler, and is open every weeknight from midnight to about 8am.

The wonderful thing about the Seaport is that it's so unlike the rest of New

Sidewalk dining in Little Italy

York. It's spacious, quaint, friendly, clean, and a heck of a lot slower. The cobblestone streets are made for strolling, arm in arm if possible, and the shops are great for browsing. Probably the best place to start looking around is **Schermerhorn Row**, on Fulton between Front and South streets, with a branch of the Strand Bookshop, a downtown installment of Laura Ashley, and free Seaport maps, as well as other handy information at the **Museum Visitor Center** (12 Fulton St). You'll find a terrific collection of books on maritime subjects at the museum shop, and nautically-themed stationery at Bowne & Co, a 19th-century printing shop at nearby 211 Water Street.

There are more retail outlets inside the Fulton Market Building, but the shopping gets really serious over at **Pier 17**, overlooking the East River. Highlights include crazy gadgets at **The Sharper Image**, and insect art at **Mariposa**.

If you're not in the mood for shopping, it might be because you're ready for lunch.

Italian waiters braced for the rush

Immediate options include **Gianni's** (15 Fulton St), which cooks up a hefty selection of pizza and pasta; **North Star Pub** (93 South St), a lively bar and restaurant; and **Sloppy Louie's** (92 South St), an old-time favorite for fish. There are plenty of others to choose from, so take a look around before you decide. Or, if you'd rather pass on a sit-down meal, both the Fulton Market Building and the third floor of Pier 17 are crammed with food stalls selling everything from simple hot dogs and fries to spare ribs and egg rolls.

After you have eaten, head up to the third-floor deck of Pier 17 for the city's best view of the **Brooklyn Bridge**. There are usually lounge chairs here, for kicking back and relaxing – this may be the best place in the whole city for a post-prandial snooze.

If you've still got energy to spare, take a tour of the Seaport's historic sloops, tugs and schooners moored at piers 16 and 15. Tickets for tours – as well as cruises of lower New York Harbor – are sold at the Pier 16 ticket booth, and at the Visitors' Center on Fulton Street.

Your downtown tour can continue with dinner in **Little Italy**, one of Manhattan's smallest and most tradition-bound neighborhoods. Wedged between Chinatown and SoHo, this has been an Italian enclave since the late 1800s, when large waves of immigrants arrived in New York from Italy. Many of the restaurants and bakeries along **Mulberry Street**, north of Canal Street, date from this time – including **Luna's** (112 Mulberry), run by the same family since 1879. Another recommendation is **Benito 1** (174 Mulberry St), which specializes in Sicilian dishes.

Umberto's Clam House (129 Mulberry St) is famed more as the place where a mafioso named Joey Gallo was gunned down in 1972 than for its cuisine, but it continues to be a popular late-night hangout. A better choice for dinner perhaps would be the **Grotta Azzurra**, a tiny basement room at the corner of Mulberry and Broome Street that serves mouth-watering Southern Italian specialties. Start off with a big pitcher of wine, a pile of garlic bread and an order of fried calamari – the rest of the meal is up to you, but try to save dessert and coffee for the next stop on this itinerary – Greenwich Village.

Hop a cab up to the lively corner of Bleecker and MacDougal Street in **Greenwich Village**. This is main street, Village-style, just a few steps from the old **Provincetown Playhouse**, where Eugene O'Neill first set the dramatic world on fire, and the **Minetta Tavern**, where Ernest Hemingway was known to hoist a few. I recommend you sit down for cappuccino and dessert at **Le Figaro** on Bleecker or **Caffe Reggio** on MacDougal, then step around the corner for a nightcap of live performances by some of the world's great jazz artists at the **Blue Note** (131 W. 3rd St).

Alternatively you may want to end your evening by checking out the blues/folk/rock scene at **The Bitter End** (149 Bleecker St) and the **Bottom Line** (15 W. 4th St), a pair of Village landmarks where shows don't even begin to get going until about 10pm.

Unwind with some late-night jazz

A half-day tour beginning with breakfast at the Carnegie Deli, then a visit to the Museum of Modern Art. A tour of Radio City Music Hall is followed by a late lunch at La Bonne Soupe.

Simply put, the **Museum of Modern Art** (MoMA) has the finest collection of late 19th and 20th-century art in the country. Not long ago, recent multi-million dollar renovation doubled the old museum's exhibition space, and although some critics bemoaned the loss of intimacy, MoMA still offers one of the most enjoyable art-experiences in the city.

The key to it all, of course, is a magnificent collection – Picasso, Matisse, Van Gogh, Monet, Pollack – are represented here, often by their most important works. In addition to the permanent collection, MoMA hosts a full calendar of special exhibitions that bring art-lovers to the museum in droves, especially on weekends. Give a call first (708-9480) to find out what's showing.

The museum opens at 11am from Saturday to Tuesday, and at noon on Thursday and Friday (closed Wednesday), so plan on a late breakfast. The **Carnegie Deli** (854 Seventh Ave) is a classic. It may be noisy and crowded but the food is good. Try the pastrami and eggs, the rich french toast, or an old standby, bagels, cream cheese and lox. Everything here is gloriously (and fatteningly) excessive. Order a deluxe platter and you'll see what I mean. One other thing: the Carnegie isn't exactly what you would call an intimate dining

The Carnegie Deli

Matisse's 'Dance'

experience. Everybody eats together at a long table. Running elbows with the natives is an essential part of the experience. And they don't accept credit cards.

If you prefer a little more breathing room with your ham and eggs, give the **Broadway Diner** a try (1726 Broadway). It's an Art Deco rehab popular with the theater crowd.

Both restaurants are located near 55th Street, so after breakfast take 55th one or two blocks back to Sixth Avenue. The signs will say Avenue of the Americas, but don't be fooled. To New Yorkers, Sixth Avenue is Sixth Avenue, no matter how many flags hang in the street. Turn right at Sixth, walk south two blocks and then turn left (east) at 53rd Street. The museum is halfway down the block.

Admission to MoMA is $9.50 ($6.50 for students and seniors) and it's worth every penny. On the ground floor, the sculpture garden features Picasso's *She Goat* and Rodin's *Monument to Balzac*, while the second floor's paintings and sculpture includes a fine selection of Picassos, plus Van Gogh's *Starry Nights*, Monet's magnificent *Water Lilies* and the gleeful *Dance* by Matisse, among many other famous works.

Be sure to catch the photography collection before moving on to the third floor's pop art extravaganza, with Warhol's familiar *Gold Marilyn* and Jasper John's *Flag*. You'll also find several pieces by Edward Hopper, as well as Andrew Wyeth's *Christina's World*, a painting that's practically an American icon.

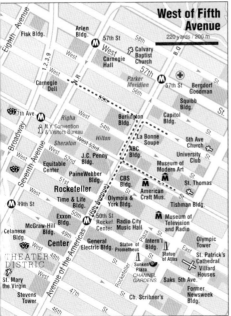

The museum's fourth floor is devoted to design and industrial art; the collection of chairs, hair dryers, lamps and assorted appliances here may seem a little eccentric, but give it a chance: you'll never look at a common object the same way again.

If you still have time, you may want to take in a film from the museum's archives, one of the best year-round film series in the city. Ask for the daily schedule and free tickets at the information desk in the

lobby. The museum also offers daily gallery talks.

Make sure you stop at the Museum Design Store across the street and the Museum Store Annex next door. Some New Yorkers come here for the shopping alone.

Across from MoMA, the **American Craft Museum**, 40 W. 53rd St (Tuesday, Wednesday, Friday to Sunday 10am–5pm, Thursday 10am–8pm; admission $5) is an airy setting for eclectic works in various mediums. For a taste of vintage New York City showbiz, instead, walk down three blocks to **Radio City Music Hall**, which stands in all its glory at the corner of Sixth and 50th Street, across from the Time-Life Building. The world's largest indoor theater – and adjacent Rockefeller Center's crowning glory – the Hall is the last word in Art Deco extravagance, from the two-ton chandeliers in the **Grand Lobby** to the plush auditorium. Even the restrooms are customized, although the Stuart Davis mural that once graced the men's smoking lounge has since been installed at the Museum of Modern Art.

The best way to experience Radio City is to attend a performance – especially the Christmas extravaganza featuring the Rockettes, the precision dance troupe that's been kicking their heels up since opening day in 1932. Otherwise, try to catch one of the backstage tours. They're about an hour long, cost $13.75 ($9 for children aged 12 and under) and usually leave every half hour, depending on the theater's schedule (for show information, call 247-4777; for tours, 632-4041).

There's more entertainment available up at **52nd Street**, where the block between Sixth and Fifth avenues is also known as 'Swing Street,' in honor of a distant past when it was lined by a bevy of jazz clubs and speakeasies (the only survivor of the latter is the venerable '21 Club,' a bar and restaurant favored by the upper crust). Nearby, the **Museum of Television and Radio**, 25 W. 52nd St (Tuesday to Sunday noon–6pm, until 8pm on Thursday; admission $6 for adults, $4 for students, and $3 for children under 13) is home to every single episode of *I Love Lucy*, among other cul-

tural landmarks and exhibits. Indulge in nostalgia at a video console until your stomach says it's time for either a late lunch or early dinner, then head back to Sixth Avenue.

Walk up three blocks back up to 55th Street and turn right. **La Bonne Soupe** (48 W. 55th St), an intimate French bistro perfect for post-museum dining, is on the right halfway down the block.

Radio City Music Hall

The Garden Court at the Frick

2. Old Masters and Polar Bears

A stroll past Millionaire's Row on Fifth Avenue, followed by a tour of the Frick Collection and a visit to the Central Park Wildlife Conservation Center.

Start your tour on Fifth Avenue and 79th Street, the beginning of the old Millionaire's Row that lies between here and 60th Street or so. Modelled after European palaces, most of these homes were built in the first quarter of the 20th century by rich industrialists. Today, many have been taken over by various cultural and civic institutions.

Among the houses to keep an eye out for is a branch of the **French Embassy** (972 Fifth Avenue), an Italian Renaissance mansion with an intricate granite facade originally built for financier Payne Whitney. The **New York University Institute of Fine Arts** (1 E. 78th St) occupies the former James B Duke mansion, modelled after an 18th-century French château; another Italian-style *palazzo*, now housing the **Commonwealth Funds** (1 E. 75th St), was built in 1909 for Edward Harkness, heir to the Standard Oil fortune; and the Lycée Français (7 E. 72nd St) now operates out of two Beaux Arts townhouses.

The mansion at the corner of Fifth Avenue and 70th Street is the **Frick Collection** (Tuesday to Saturday 10am –6pm, Sunday 1–6pm, closed Monday; admission $5), built in 1914 by

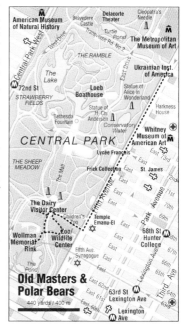

Henry Clay Frick, whose passion for acquiring art was surpassed only by his ruthlessness in business. The collection, which is made up almost entirely of European paintings and furnishings from the 16th to 19th centuries, represents one of the city's most successful combinations of art and environment. The ambience is of quiet (and to some minds somewhat stultifying) gentility, with gracious touches like soft chairs to sink into. An effort has been made to retain a warm, non-institutional feeling, and it clearly pays off. You'll probably want to spend at least a couple of hours at the Frick; be sure to leave plenty of time for the central courtyard, a soothing respite from the city streets.

Leaving the Frick, continue walking down Fifth Avenue, taking note of the stately **Lotos Club** (5 E. 66th St) and the enormous **Temple Emanu-El** (1 E. 65th St). Turn right at the 65th Street entrance to Central Park, walk around the imposing Arsenal, which now houses the the city's parks administration headquarters, and enter the **Central Park Wildlife Conservation Center**.

It's difficult to imagine that there are polar bears and monkeys in the middle of Manhattan's concrete jungle, but there are. And of all places, just off Fifth Avenue. Be warned before you pay your dollar, this is not one of the world's grandest zoos, although considering its modest size and resources it might be one of the most successful. A while ago, a $35 million renovation replaced the old steel cages with simulated habitats, and in some cases the only thing between the spectators and the animals are glass walls between outcroppings of rock. There are also several good indoor exhibits including a glass-enclosed penguin tank, a nifty polar bear swimming pool, and a tiny tropical rainforest with free-flying birds.

Zoo favorite

If you're feeling hungry, grab a bite at the Zoo Cafe, or a hot dog from one of the ubiquitous vendors, then follow signs (or ask directions) to **The Dairy**, aka the Central Park Visitor Center, which houses special exhibits along with helpful maps and information about park tours and events. While you are here, stop by and watch the carousel's 58 hand-carved horses go round, or in winter take a spin on the ice at the **Wollman Rink**.

3. A Walk on the West Side

A morning option beginning with breakfast or brunch on the Upper West Side, followed by a tour of the American Museum of Natural History and shopping on Columbus Avenue.

If you're traveling with children, the **American Museum of Natural History** (10am–5.45pm, until 8.45pm Friday and Saturday; recommended voluntary admission fee $8 for adults, $4.50 for children), a lumpy, lumbering giant that takes up four blocks on Central Park West between 77th and 81st streets, is an absolute must, if only for the dinosaur exhibit. That's not to say this is a kids-only venture. With some 30 million artifacts and specimens on display in 22 interconnected buildings, there's plenty for grown-ups to see too. But be selective. Don't even think about doing the whole place in one shot. Two or three hours should be sufficient, an extra hour if you also visit the Planetarium or Naturemax Theater.

Follow the sign

Begin the day at **Good Enough to Eat** (483 Amsterdam Avenue, near W. 83rd St), a cozy restaurant that serves up tasty egg dishes with fresh scones, muffins and strawberry butter. Nearby, another **Sarabeth's Kitchen** (423 Amsterdam, near 81st St) offers a comfortable atmosphere for breakfast or brunch, with lots of transplanted country atmosphere along with generous portions of delicious food.

From 83rd Street, walk over to Central Park West, turn right and

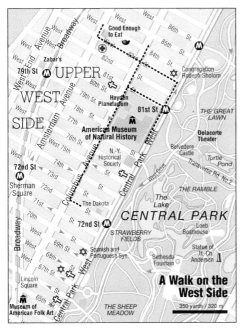

continue three blocks to the main entrance to the museum, guarded by an equestrian statue of Theodore Roosevelt. The old facade – a stately Romanesque arcade with two elaborate towers – was built in 1892 and is still visible around the corner on 77th Street.

Enter the museum and head to the fourth-floor dinosaur exhibits, recently reinstalled in six renovated halls. The prehistoric celebrities mounted here offer an astounding look at life

on earth in eons past. Elsewhere in the museum, exhibition space is divided between biology and anthropology.

There are too many exhibits to describe individually, but there are a few you should really try to catch. On the third floor, be sure to stop at the **Pacific Peoples** and **Plains Indians** galleries. The exhibits give a balanced mix of material objects and cultural analysis, with recorded commentary, music and sound effects creating the appropriate atmosphere. There's an interesting collection of pre-Columbian clay figures on the second floor in addition to reproductions of the Aztec sun stone, a massive Olmec head and two 35-ft (10-meter) stelae. On the first floor, the **Northwest Coast Indians** exhibit features a 65-ft (19-meter) Chilkat canoe as well as a fine collection of totem poles and other ritual art. A full-scale model of a blue whale hangs in the **Hall of Ocean Life**, and the **Biology of Man** exhibit does a good job exploring human evolution and genetics. Check out the 34-ton meteorite around the corner at the **Hall of Meteorites** and the famous Star of India – the largest blue sapphire in the world – at the adjoining **Minerals and Gems Gallery**.

Admission to the museum's **IMAX Theater** is an additional $9 on Friday and Saturday evenings, when the dazzling laser light shows formerly running at the Hayden Planetarium are presented here while a new Center for Earth and Space is under construction (it's scheduled to open in 2000). Naturemax films – projected on a screen four stories high and 66ft (20m) wide – are presented several times daily and cost $12 for adults and $6.50 for children, a fee which includes admission to the museum.

From the museum, turn left on West 81st St, and cross over to **Columbus Avenue**. Like Madison Avenue, Columbus is committed to mass consumption. If you haven't seen enough bones already, stop at **Maxilla and Mandible**, just past 81st Street, one of two stores in New York that sells human and animal skeletons. Nearby, **Frank Stella** offers classy menswear; beyond 83rd Street, **Handblock/April Cornell** carries hand-printed Indian fabrics.

At this point, stop, take a deep breath and think about something that's really important – what to eat for lunch. Just beyond 84th Street, **Panarella's** (513 Columbus) specializes in Northern Italian cuisine. If you crave a meal with a country-western kick, turn around and walk south on Columbus.

A few blocks down, turn left for **Dallas BBQ** (27 W. 72nd), a crowded, casual spot that serves up simple, hearty ribs, chicken, burgers and crispy onions. Enroute you'll pass the **IS 44 Flea Market** (Sunday only) at 77th Street, where there's more old – and some new – stuff for sale.

4. Shopping Safari

Midtown's major department stores, with a short detour up Madison Avenue, followed by lunch (or dinner).

New York has the greatest department stores in the world. The variety is unrivaled, the quality is top-notch, and although prices may be higher than what you're used to, there's no telling when you'll stumble on a drop-dead bargain.

The following itinerary gives a run-down of the best department stores in Manhattan. It's virtually impossible to go to each one in the span of a single morning, so select a few that sound right for you. Macy's, Saks Fifth Avenue and Bloomingdale's are probably the three essentials, but serious shoppers may want to narrow it down to two – or even one.

Marvelous Macy's

Walk or hop a cab to **Macy's**, on Seventh Avenue between 34th and 35th streets, in the heart of the Garment District. Keep an eye out for the young men pushing clothes racks in the street. They've been known to run down a pedestrian or two.

Like the billboard says, Macy's is the biggest department store in the world, and it's worth seeing for its size alone. Once a staple for middle-class shoppers, these days it's giving even upscale stores a run for their money. Don't leave without walking through the **Cellar**, a gourmet emporium with every culinary do-dad an imaginative chef could ask for.

Leave Macy's from the Broadway exit and cross Herald Square, a sliver of concrete where Broadway intersects Sixth Avenue. The nearby Manhattan Mall shopping plaza (100 West 33rd St) might provide some diversion before you continue along 34th Street to Fifth Avenue. The Empire State Building is at the corner.

Lord & Taylor, five blocks up Fifth Avenue at 39th Street, caters to the

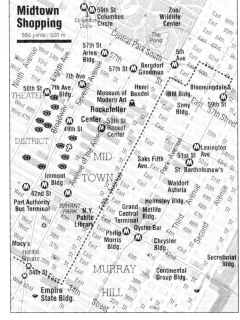

Midtown Shopping map: 550 yards / 500 m. Includes locations such as Columbus Circle, 59th St, Central Park South, 57th St, Bergdorf Goodman, Henri Bendel, Museum of Modern Art, IBM Bldg., Sony Bldg., Bloomingdale's, Rockefeller Center, Radio City, Lexington Ave, Saks Fifth Ave., St. Bartholomew's, Theater District, Times Square, Waldorf Astoria, Helmsley Bldg., Metlife Bldg., Grand Central Terminal, Port Authority Bus Terminal, Bryant Park, N.Y. Public Library, Philip Morris Bldg., Oyster Bar, Chrysler Bldg., Immont Bldg., Macy's, Herald Square, Empire State Bldg., Murray Hill, Continental Group Bldg., Secretariat Bldg., Zoo/Wildlife Center, The Pond.

Toys galore at F.A.O. Schwarz

Establishment. Of all the department stores on Fifth Avenue, Lord & Taylor is most famous for its lavish displays, especially around Christmas when people line up just to peer through the windows.

Farther up Fifth, at 50th Street, **Saks Fifth Avenue** aims at the same traditional tastes but adds an extra measure of prestige. You may have shopped at Saks stores elsewhere in the country, but nothing beats the original for elegance. The store has an added appeal for some: there's a good chance of bumping into a celebrity or two.

If you're in need of refreshment, stop at **Takashimaya** (683 Fifth Avenue, near 55th St), which offers a serene basement tea room, along with upper floors stocked with interesting clothing and furniture. Across the street, **Henri Bendel** (712 Fifth Ave) is not a department store so much as an overgrown boutique, geared toward a hipper, more adventurous clientele than most stores.

If you haven't already, stop in for a gawk at the jewels, silver and crystal goblets at **Tiffany & Co.**, at the southeast corner of 57th Street, before continuing to 58th Street and **Bergdorf Goodman**. The store is located next door to the Plaza Hotel on the former site of the Cornelius Vanderbilt mansion, and the air of opulence has clearly lingered. Bergdorf is more like a collection of small boutiques than a department store. The atmosphere is refined, the racks are filled with unique designer fashions, and the prices...well, as the saying goes, if you have to ask, you can't afford it.

New York's ultimate toy store, **F.A.O. Schwarz**, across Fifth Avenue, inside the sprawling General Motors Building at 767 Fifth Avenue. During the Christmas shopping season, you will find lines of people waiting to get inside. Take a quick peek for yourself before heading east on 58th Street to Madison Avenue. A short walk north brings you to the understated elegance of **Calvin Klein**, followed by the uptown branch of **Barneys New York**, between 60th and 61st streets. (The original of this bastion of exclusive and pricey downtown fashion is at Seventh Avenue and 17th Street.)

Bloomingdale's, a New York institution

Check out the designer wear, the shoes, the bags, the attitude and then have lunch at **Fred's**, the store's immensely popular lower-level trattoria. If you can't get a table here, try **Madame Romaine de Lyon** (132 E. 61st St), a welcoming bistro that serves at least 100 kinds of omelette. (Alternatively, see the options listed at the end of this tour.)

Keep walking east on 61st Street until you reach Lexington Avenue: **Bloomingdale's**, a minor institution that most true-blue New Yorkers couldn't do without, is on the next block down. Style and quality are a given trademark at Bloomies, and the prices, although high, are still somewhere in the ballpark, although which deck is debatable. It is usually crowded, especially during holiday sales, but if you only go to one store in New York, this should be it. If Bloomingdale's doesn't have what you're looking for, the item probably doesn't exist.

If you still haven't eaten lunch, there's a cluster of good restaurants near or on the corner of Third Avenue and 60th Street. **Yellowfingers** (200 E. 60th St) and **Contrapunto**, upstairs, are both good for pastas, salads and light entrées, while both the **Arizona 206** and **café** (206 E. 60th St) specialize in innovative dishes with a southwestern twist.

However, if you have energy to spare, pass this trio up and trek to 74th Street and Third, where **J.G. Melon**, a small, cozy restaurant and pub, is a great spot for burgers and beer. A little further uptown, the airier **Mezzaluna** (1295 Third Ave) specializes in pizza and pasta.

5. Capitalism in Action

A visit to the New York Stock Exchange, Federal Hall, Trinity Church, St Paul's Chapel and City Hall, followed by lunch in Chinatown.

Bowling Green, located in a cobbled plaza at the foot of Broadway, is the city's oldest space. The statue of King George III that once stood here was torn down by a mob in 1776 after a reading of the Declaration of Independence worked them into a frenzy. The statue was melted down into musket balls, supposedly shot at British troops. The iron fence around the park dates from 1771.

The leafy Bowling Green

Facing the plaza from the south is the former US Custom House, a fabulously ornate structure designed by Cass Gilbert and completed

Action on the floor

in 1907. In 1994, the George Gustav Heye Center of the **National Museum of the American Indian** (daily 10am–5pm) opened here. Admission is free and exhibits offer an in-depth appreciation of Native American culture, identity and beliefs. From here, head up Broadway to Wall Street, named after the wood fence erected by Dutch colonists to keep their British neighbors at arm's length. Trinity Church is now immediately to your left, the steep stairway of Federal Hall is across the street, and the New York Stock Exchange is down and to the right.

Walk two blocks down Wall Street, turn right at Broad, and enter the **New York Stock Exchange** (NYSE), an imposing Classical temple built in 1903. The action on the trading floor usually runs hot and heavy, with traders yelling, computers flashing and papers flying every which way – capitalism in action; a roller-coaster of buying and selling that keeps most American corporations in business.

Tickets to the NYSE are free but limited. If the **Visitor Center** is booked up – and it usually is – a NYSE staffer will be at the door handing out tickets. You may have to wait about an hour, so in the meanwhile, double back for a look at Federal Hall and Trinity Church.

Federal Hall is a splendid Greek Revival mansion built in 1842 on the former site of the British City Hall. George Washington was inaugurated at the site in 1789; the statue at the top of the steps commemorates the event. Inside Federal Hall, there are changing exhibits on government and law which are mostly of interest to history-buffs.

Across Broadway, the Gothic façade of **Trinity Church** stares down Wall Street like an admonishing nun – a poignant reminder to all those fast-dealing arbitrators that earthly deeds have heav-

enly consequences. The church is surrounded by one of the city's oldest cemeteries. Some of the historic figures buried here include Alexander Hamilton, who was killed in a duel with Aaron Burr, and Robert Fulton, who was the inventor of the steamship that ferried passengers between South Street and Brooklyn.

While you're in the neighborhood, you might

Federal Hall

want to poke your head into **1 Wall Street** (The Bank of New York), just across Broadway. It's an Art Deco treasure with a rippling gray facade and a brilliant red and gold mosaic lobby. You might also want to take a look at the **Morgan Guaranty Trust Company** (23 Wall St), still scarred by a mysterious explosion set off in 1920 which killed 33 people, injured hundreds, and shattered windows as much as 10 blocks away.

When you're done nosing around Wall Street, continue walking up Broadway about another six blocks to **St Paul's Chapel**, the city's oldest church, built in 1766. St Paul's is far more modest than Trinity, reflecting the earlier Georgian style, but it too has a peaceful graveyard behind the chapel with a collection of beautifully carved headstones. With the World Trade Center looming overhead and traffic buzzing on all four sides, the church makes a strange but soothing resting place.

The **Woolworth Building** is another two blocks up Broadway at number 233. This is F. W. Woolworth's monument to himself, an ornate Gothic tower adorned with allegorical figures, gargoyles and a stunning marble lobby. The five-and-dime king commissioned Cass Gilbert to design the building, and paid over $13 million in cash to see that it was done right. It was completed in 1913 and for 16 years was the tallest building in the world.

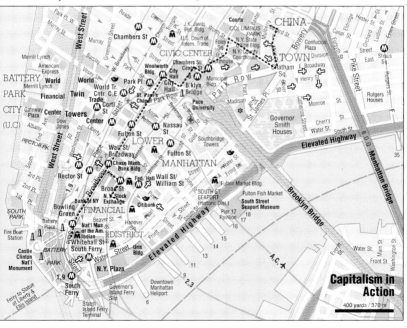

Capitalism in Action

400 yards / 370 m

Chinatown: a great place to eat

From the Woolworth Building, cross Broadway and head uptown through City Hall Park, past the entrance to the Brooklyn Bridge. Be sure to get a good look at **City Hall** itself, an elegant Federal mansion completed in 1811. City Hall is backed by the New York City Courthouse, better known as the Tweed Courthouse because Boss Tweed and his cronies pocketed millions in kickbacks during its construction.

Continue straight up Center Street into Foley Square, passing the Municipal Building and US Court House. Turn right at Worth Street, walk three blocks to Mott and turn left into **Chinatown**.

One of countless options

It is estimated that half of New York's 300,000 Chinese residents live in this vibrant, growing neighborhood, which got its start over a century ago in the three-block area bordered by Mott, Pell and the Bowery. The best place to start exploring is the **Museum of Chinese in the Americas** (70 Mulberry St). It's hardly surprising that most New Yorkers just come here to eat, however. There are so many wonderful restaurants crowded into this corner of Chinatown, it's hard to choose between them. If it's your first visit, you might want to stick with **Mandarin Court** (61 Mott St), known for its friendly atmosphere and excellent dim sum. If you are feeling a little more adventurous, keep walking up Mott Street to **Vegetarian's Paradise**, **Peking Duck**, or a cheap little noodle house called **Wo Hop**. If none of them appeal, walk over to the **Bowery**, where both the **HSF** (46) and the large and bustling **Silver Palace** (50) are extremely popular. Be assured no matter where you end up, the food will be tasty, fairly inexpensive and plentiful.

6. Harlem

Get a new perspective on this historic African-American neighborhood with a guided tour of local markets, churches and landmark buildings.

Because of Harlem's reputation, many travelers don't consider making a visit. Most people know only what they see on the news – devastated streets, drug gangs, abandoned buildings, hopelessness – all part of Harlem life, but by no means the whole story. Amid the desolation there are vital African-American and Hispanic communities, and important architectural and historic sights. There are also new investments such as Harlem USA, a five-story mall complex on W. 125th St that includes an HMV music store and a Disney store. Even a casual survey of Manhattan would be incomplete without at least a brief tour of Harlem. And of course, for travelers with a particular interest in black American culture, a visit to Harlem is absolutely essential.

Bagging bargains in Harlem

Harlem's attractions are too far apart for a walking tour, and frankly, wandering around without a guide is not recommended. Your best bet is to sign on with one of the sightseeing companies that specialize in upper Manhattan. Both Harlem Spirituals (tel: 757-0425) and Harlem Your Way! (tel: 690-1687) offer tours designed to give a rounded view of Harlem – its troubles and its successes. Be sure to call for reservations at least two days in advance. The best time to pay a visit is Sunday morning, when a rousing gospel service at a local Baptist church is usually included in the tour.

Among the sights covered by the tours are the handsome townhouses designed by Stanford White at **Strivers Row** and **Sugar Hill**; the **Hamilton Heights Historic District**, where Alexander Hamilton, the country's first Secretary of the Treasury lived; the **Abyssinian Baptist Church** where Adam Clayton Powell, Jr launched his career; and **La Marqueta**, a market in **Spanish Harlem** with all kinds of tropical fruits and spices for sale. For many people the highlight of a tour of Harlem is the **Apollo Theater** (tel: 222-0992), which has launched so many musical careers, including those of Ella Fitzgerald, James Brown and Michael Jackson.

Most tours include lunch, but if you have a choice, head to **Sylvia's** (328 Lenox Avenue, near 127th St) for real soul food.

An afternoon tour of Lincoln Center, followed by a walk along Riverside Drive. Return via upper Broadway to Lincoln Center in time for an evening performance, followed by dinner at a nearby restaurant.

Start the afternoon at **Lincoln Center**, New York's premier address for the performing arts. Built in the early 1960s as part of a massive redevelopment plan intended to clean up the slum that used to occupy the site, the complex is flanked on one side by the **Julliard School** and on the other by a branch of **Fordham University**. A word of warning: don't expect to buy same-day tickets for a performance. Although standing room and cancellations are sometimes available

Julliard School

a few hours before curtain time, your best bet is to reserve seats in advance. If possible, order them over the phone before coming to New York. For schedules and prices, tel: 875-5400.

Guided tours of the complex are given every hour between 10.30am and 5.30pm (tel: 875-5350 for exact times).

Standing at the black marble fountain in the middle of the plaza, you are surrounded by the glass and white marble facades of Lincoln Center's three main structures. The **Metropolitan Opera** is directly in front. Two large murals by Marc Chagall hang behind the glass wall – *Le Triomphe de la Musique* to the left, *Les Sources de la Musique* to the right. The Met is home to the Metropolitan Opera Company from October to April and the American Ballet Theater from April to June. Its lavish productions and big-name performers carry a hefty price tag. Seats run anywhere between $20 and $100, depending on where you sit and what's playing.

To the left of the central fountain, the **New York State Theater** is shared by the New York City Opera

A Night at the Opera

350 yards / 320 m

West Side Highway (Miller Highway)

Riverside Drive

West End Avenue

Amsterdam Avenue

Columbus Avenue

Central Park West

Broadway

Freedom Pl

Zabar's

West 79th St

UPPER
WEST
SIDE

Hayden Planetarium

American Museum of Natural History

N.-Y. Historical Society

72nd St

Sherman Square

The Dakota

72nd St

Lincoln Towers

Stev's Towers

Con-Edison

Julliard School

A.Tully Hall

Spanish and Portuguese Syn.

V. Beaumont Theater

Amsterdam Houses

Metropolitan Opera

Avery Fisher Hall

Lincoln Square

CENTRAL PARK

Lincoln Center

Museum of American Folk Art

N.Y. State Theater

Fordham University

THE SHEEP MEADOW

Transverse Rd No 1

and Ballet. Both tend to be more adventurous than the Met and offer tickets at about half the price. If the doors are open, take a look at Jasper Johns' painting on the ground floor and the two controversial marble statues by Elie Nadelman displayed in the upstairs foyer.

The third side of the main plaza is occupied by **Avery Fisher Hall**, home of the New York Philharmonic and the popular Mostly Mozart series held in July and August. Peek in for a look at Richard Lippold's *Orpheus and Apollo*, a hanging metal sculpture that dominates the foyer.

Two secondary courtyards flank the Met. To the right, the **Vivian Beaumont Theater** and the **New York Public Library for the Performing Arts** are fronted by a shady plaza and reflecting pool where brown-baggers gather for lunch. Henry Moore's oxidized bronze sculpture is in the center of the pool. A spindly steel sculpture by Alexander Calder is near the library entrance. **Damrosch Park** is located to the left. The Guggenheim Bandshell at the far end is used for free concerts during summer, usually around lunchtime and in the early evening.

Leaving Lincoln Center, head across the street to the **Museum of American Folk Art** (2 Lincoln Square), for exhibits on everything from Amish quilts to Shaker furniture. The gift shop next door is a virtual wonderland of small, inexpensive *chotckas* for the folks back home – and the museum is open Tuesday to Sunday 11.30am –7.30pm. Admission is free. From here, walk up to 66th Street, where Columbus Avenue veers to the right. Keep left on Broadway.

When you get to 72nd Street, turn left for a quick look at high-class living on the Upper West Side. Walk all the way down to Riverside Drive, winding along the edge of Frederick Law Olmsted's Riverside Park. Turn right and walk as far as 81st Street. This is one of the most picturesque corners of the island, with exceptional architecture and sweeping views of the **Hudson River**. Be sure to look at the houseboats at the 79th Street Boat Basin, where a few salty Manhattanites brave the elements all year round.

A favorite Riverside pastime

Gourmets' choice

Turn right at 81st Street, walk two blocks to Broadway, and turn right again heading back toward Lincoln Center. This section of Broadway is a 24-hour stage, the one place where all the incongruities of the Upper West Side flow clamorously together.

In general, the shopping isn't as rich here as on Columbus, but Broadway is a gourmet's mecca. For example, **Zabar's** (at the corner of 80th Street) is the food delicacy shop against which all others are measured (apologies to Balducci's downtown). Some people would pay just to get in. Even if you are not in the mood for buying, it's a kick just looking around or elbowing your way up to the counters for a free taste of all the high-calorie goodies.

A stone's throw from Zabar's, **H&H Bagels** make over 60,000 every day, should you ever find yourself in dire need of one smothered in cream cheese. Meanwhile **Barnes and Noble** offers coffee and thousands of books for sale back at 82nd Street

Farther down Broadway, the **Ansonia Hotel**, a residential apartment building, occupies the entire block between 73rd and 74th streets. Although a bit worn around the edges, this is the grand dame of West Side apartment buildings with a guest list that once included Enrico Caruso, Igor Stravinsky, Arturo Toscanini and Theodore Dreiser. Although retailers have decimated the ground floor, the Ansonia's mansard roof, corner towers and terracotta detailing still add up to a Beaux Arts fantasy that captures the gaze and refuses to let go.

The Met at night

If time permits you can catch a cab here back to your hotel in order to freshen up before evening. Otherwise, continue past the tangled intersection with Columbus Avenue, maybe stopping for a pre-performance espresso at one of the chic little cafes directly across from Lincoln Center.

After the performance, your choice of nearby dinner venues is virtually limitless: for reasonably priced sushi, try **Lenge** (202 Columbus Ave) or **Rikyu** (210 Columbus Ave); for upscale French bistro food, definitely book ahead at **Cafe Luxembourg** (200 W. 70th). And, for post-dinner jazz in surreal surroundings, the **Iridium** jazz club (44 W. 63rd St) is right next door to Lincoln Center.

A tour of Times Square, followed by a Broadway show and dinner at a nearby restaurant.

The New York theater is famed world-wide. With good reason. Although Broadway has had its ups and downs, the the Great White Way – so named because in the early part of the 20th century it was lit by bright white electric lights – continues to draw crowds to such long-running productions as *Les Misérables* and *Cats*. Rare is the visitor who doesn't include dinner and a Broadway show as part of their itinerary.

A word about theater tickets: If you want to avoid waiting in line, it's best to order them by phone or else drop into the box office of the particular theater ahead of time; be prepared for prices as high as $75 for the latest hits.

If you're looking for a bargain, start your visit at the TKTS booth at 47th Street and Broadway, just north of Times Square, where theater tickets are discounted by 50 to 75 percent. It's open 3–8pm, and on Wednesdays and Saturdays (for matinee performances)10am–2pm; Sundays from noon until closing. You may have to wait in line,

In Times Square

but the crowd is usually interesting and chatty and the savings make it well worthwhile.

Compared to Broadway's peak in the 1920s, when as many as 250 shows a year were produced by legendary producers like the Schubert brothers and David Belasco, today's average of 30 or so new productions a year may seem paltry. Still, many are staged in the

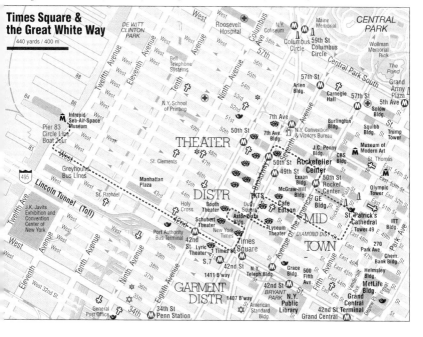

Times Square & the Great White Way

440 yards / 400 m

same grand old venues. From the TKTS booth, walk south two blocks to 45th Street and turn left for the **Lyceum**, the oldest theater on Broadway, and with its elaborate baroque facade and dramatic mansard roof, one of the most beautiful. Double back on 45th Street, cross Broadway, and walk down to Schubert Alley, which runs behind the **Booth** and **Schubert** theaters, both built in 1913. **Sardi's** restaurant, the traditional first-night watering hole for actors and producers, is right across the street.

One of the best views of **Times Square** (especially stunning on New Year's Eve, when the famous ball drops) can be had from the New York Marriott Marquis Hotel's revolving rooftop restaurant. The sprawling, 50-story edifice, on Broadway between 45th and 46th streets, was one of the first new properties to open in the area, which now boasts a whopping 15 percent of New York City's hotels, including the high-tech **Paramount**, with interiors designed by Philippe Starck, on restaurant-packed West 46th Street.

The neon heart of Manhattan, Times Square was actually named for the *New York Times*, once headquartered in the Times Tower at the intersection of 42nd Street and Seventh Avenue. (The building, site of the world's first moving sign, still stands, but the paper has moved around the corner.) Thanks to over 40 illuminated billboards and signs, this part of town literally shines at night: in fact the ongoing clean-up of the 'crossroads of the world' has attracted new businesses like the All Star Cafe and the Virgin Megastore, both on Broadway between 45th and 46th streets, along with investors like Disney and Madame Tussaud's. Still it's worth noting that Times Square also attracts pickpockets and hustlers, which means that the usual precautions apply: keep you wallet in your front pocket, and hold on to your purse.

A walk west on 42nd Street between Seventh and Eighth avenues takes you past a row of turn-of-the-century theaters, including the renovated **New Victory**. The **Visitor Center**, currently in the Selwyn Theater at 229 West 42nd Street, offers brochures and maps of the city, as well as free tours of Times Square on Fridays.

These days, most of the area's remaining porno shops and sex shows are clustered along Eighth Avenue by the Port Authority Bus Terminal, which means you may want to avoid this area. Instead, grab a cab to the **Intrepid Sea-Air-Space Museum** (Monday to Saturday 10am–5pm, Sunday 10am–6pm; admission $10, less for students, seniors and members of the armed forces), a World War II aircraft carrier and five other ships moored at West 46th Street and the Hudson River (Pier 86), just south of the city's Passenger Ship Terminal.

If you only have time for a quick meal before the show starts, take heart: the theater district has over 200 restaurants to choose from. For an authentic New York coffee shop experience, you can't beat the somewhat seedy **Edison Cafe**, inside the Hotel Edison (228 West 47th St), which caters to the theatrical crowd.

For speedy pre-theater service and reasonable prices, try the bistro fare at **Cafe Un Deux Trois** (123 West 44th St, east of Broadway) or the even cheaper *prix-fixe* dinner at the **Hourglass Tavern** (373 West 46th, near Ninth Avenue), where an hourglass over each table actually times the customers, who have only 60 minutes to gobble their dinner. It's a great deal for shoe-string travelers (unless of course they happen to be slow chewers).

Times Square times two

You may feel it is too early to dine and would rather a gala post-performance splurge. In this case, choose between two neighboring Italian eateries: **Orso** (322 West 46th St), where you might spot a celebrity or two; or **Barbetta** (321 West 46th St), an old-world, elegant restaurant with a garden that's been run by the same family for over nine decades.

9. United Nations and Midtown East

A visit to the United Nations followed by a walking (and eating) tour of Midtown East, including the Chrysler Building, Grand Central Station, the Waldorf-Astoria and the Sony Building.

Start your day with a morning visit to the **United Nations Headquarters**, a 'must-see' on most checklists. Spread along First Avenue between 42nd and 48th streets, with the main entrance at 46th Street, the UN cuts an impressive figure, although it doesn't have quite the architectural wallop it did 40 years ago. What's more, the guided tours tend to be a bit tedious. But if you have a

special love for international affairs, indulge yourself. Don't forget to check out the giftshop and the moon-rock display, and have breakfast in the coffee shop. If it's later in the day, and you've time to spare, have a bite at the **Delegates' Dining Room**. The clientele is fascinating and the view of the East River not bad, either (reservations are essential; so is proper attire; tel: 963-7626).

For those of you determined to

UN Headquarters

The Chrysler Building

go the whole nine yards, catch one of the guided tours in the main lobby. They leave every 30 minutes or so and generally last about 45 minutes ($7.50 for adults, $4.50 for students, last tour at 4.45pm). Visitors are occasionally allowed to watch the proceedings of the General Assembly. Ask for free tickets at the information desk.

Exit the UN and walk down to the corner of 42nd Street, where a steep stairway festooned with banners leads up to an apartment complex called **Tudor City**. You can either climb up the stairs or loop around the block. In either case, head for the **Ford Foundation Building** near the corner of 42nd Street and Second Avenue. Behind its sheer gray walls is a magnificent 12-story atrium thick with vegetation. It's one of the most peaceful places in midtown, and a triumph of interior design.

Walk west on 42nd Street and you'll come to the landmark **Daily News Building**, an Art Deco skyscraper built in 1930 – and until recently home to the newsroom of New York's largest-circulation daily (now relocated to W. 33rd St). When scouts were looking for a location to double as the *Daily Planet* building in the *Superman* movies, this is the one they chose. Pause to admire the carved-stone relief over the entrance before continuing to the **Chrysler Building**, which rises from the corner of Lexington Avenue. For a few precious months in 1930, this was the tallest building in the world, and in the hearts of some New Yorkers, it still is. Erected by auto czar Walter Chrysler, its glorious spire soars 1,000ft (304 meters) into the sky. Of all the landmarks in the city, this is the most loved, an elaborate Art Deco jewel with whimsical touches. Take a walk through the marble-wrapped lobby and get a good look at the ceiling mural and lavishly decorated elevator doors. More than a beautiful building, it's a symbol of an era, a proud classic through and through.

Continue on 42nd Street past the Grand Hyatt Hotel to **Grand Central Terminal**, a vast Beaux Arts monument housing one of the country's greatest railway stations. Enter the terminal and follow signs to the main concourse,

Grand Central Station facade

a barrel-vaulted shell 150ft (46m) high and 470ft (145m) long with enormous arched windows and about 2,500 stars painted on the ceiling. The Municipal Art Society gives free weekly tours; tel: 935-3969 for details. One of the city's unique dining experiences, the famous **Oyster Bar**, is located underground in a dramatically vaulted chamber. Leave it to New Yorkers to put one of their best restaurants in a subway station. If you're feeling hungry – heck, even if you're not – slurp down a few oysters with an ice-cold beer. Heaven knows you won't be alone. The Oyster Bar shucks more than 10,000 oysters every day.

Directly across 42nd Street, the **Philip Morris Building** houses a satellite gallery (closed weekends) of the **Whitney Museum**. It's perfect for a quick artfix before venturing into the heart of Midtown East. When you're finished at the gallery, turn left on 42nd Street and then right on **Madison Avenue**, the adrenal gland of Manhattan. This is archetypal New York – the skyline bristling with gleaming glass towers, the streets jammed with taxis, and everyone dashing crazily around like they're 20 minutes late.

At Madison and 50th Street, directly behind St Patrick's Cathedral, the graceful Renaissance-style **Villard Houses** once belonged to the Archdiocese of New York; two form the base of the **New York Palace Hotel**. One block east, the **Waldorf-Astoria Hotel** stands solidly at the corner of Park Avenue and 50th. In fact, it takes up the entire block. Like Radio City Music Hall, the Waldorf was built during the Great Depression and shares the same flair.

A walk south brings you back to Grand Central Terminal, via twin walkways through the gold-topped **Helmsley Building** that embraces the bottom of Park Avenue. Above the terminal, the **MetLife Building** – formerly the Pan-Am Building – looms over Park like a glass-plated Goliath. For a look at a more graceful modern

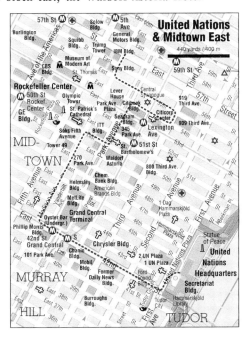

57

Citicorp Center

structure, head north (uptown) past **St Bartholomew's Church** all the way to 53rd Street.

Turn right, cross Lexington and continue to the Third Avenue entrance of **The Shops** at **Citicorp Center**. Before going in, look up. You might barely be able to see the structure's signature bevelled roof. Completed in 1979, the Citicorp Building is one of the most distinct – and distinctive – additions to the Manhattan skyline, as conspicuous from most angles as the Empire State or Chrysler buildings. There are several inviting new stores and restaurants set around an atrium, where, occasionally, musicians give free lunchtime concerts to passersby.

Exit Citicorp Center the same way you came in, getting a good look at the '**Lipstick Building**' at 54th and Third, an oval tower that challenges the straight-edged geometry of its neighbors. If you haven't eaten, try the lobby's **Lipstick Cafe**, a popular midtown spot for lunch and breakfast.

From here, walk up to 55th Street, turn left and return to Madison Avenue, where the unusually shaped **Sony Building** – built for AT&T – rises like a giant funnel. Designed by Philip Johnson, the post-modern monolith's eclectic appearance – a Chippendale top and Renaissance bottom, with a modern skyscraper in between – is an eye-catcher. And now that Sony's taken over, its echoing public plaza has been filled in with a narrow arcade of shops selling high-tech Sony equipment and gear. Be sure to stop in at the **Sony Wonder Technology Lab**, a free series of interactive exhibits and displays that's open Tuesday to Saturday 10am–6pm, Sunday noon–6pm. Kids and techies will love it (the entrance is at 56th Street).

The former **IBM Building**, another granite monolith from the 1980s, lifts off from the next corner. Now home to the Tourneau watch empire, it includes a pleasant glass-enclosed atrium-cum-sculpture garden where you can rest your feet and watch the endless passing parade.

Shopping on Orchard Street, followed by a visit to the Lower East Side Tenement Museum and a short tour of the colorful East Village.

The Lower East Side is a bargain-hunter's paradise. Die-hard shoppers can easily spend a whole day rifling through the racks on Orchard Street, and pocket-price gourmets will find no end of cholesterol-soaked goodies at classic Jewish delicatessens such as Ratners and Bernstein-on-Essex.

The traditional Lower East Side, with its Jewish roots firmly in place, slants south of East Houston Street to the East River. This is where Eastern European immigrants settled during the 19th century, and where today's savvy bargain-hunters flock for wholesale deals in everything from extravagant bridal gowns to bathroom fixtures. Sundays are the big shopping days here (stores are closed on Saturday); if crowds aren't your scene, you might want to try coming on a weekday.

Care for a salt beef sandwich?

Before you get too involved with shopping, however, put yourself in the proper frame of mind at **Yonah Schimmel's Bakery** (137 E. Houston St), near the corner of Forsyth. Don't let appearances fool you. The decor here may be strictly down-and-out, but the baked goods are out-of-this-world. Ask for a *knish* – spinach, *kasha* (cracked wheat) or classic potato – heated please, to go. With any one of these warming your belly, you'll be fuelled up for the afternoon ahead.

Turn right on East Houston and walk over to Essex Street, about six blocks away. En route, you can provision yourself for a midnight snack – a couple of doughy delights at **Moishe's Bagels**, fresh cream cheese at **Ben's Cheese Shop** and paper-thin lox (smoked salmon) at **Russ & Daughters**. Be sure to

peek into **Katz's** delicatessen, one of the neighborhood's real old-timers.

The offerings get richer, and somewhat stranger, around the corner on Essex Street. You can satisfy your sweet tooth at the **Economy Candy Market**, near the corner of Rivington Street, or turn left at Rivington for a visit to the **Schapiro Wine Company**, the only kosher winery in the city (tours and wine-tasting on Sundays). Double back to Essex and take another left, at Delancey Street, and you'll come to **Ratners** dairy restaurant, hands-down winner of the rude waiter award (and in these parts, the competition is pretty stiff). It's one of the most popular restaurants around, so you might want to try a blintz before heading back the way you came to **Orchard Street**. From here on in, you are on your own. Orchard Street is so swamped with vendors, shoppers and merchandise, it's next to impossible to guide you through the chaos. A word of advice, however. Don't be afraid to haggle. You'll never get a bargain unless you request – strike that – demand it. Be bold, be stubborn, be downright pig-headed.

Be sure to leave time for a visit to the **Lower East Side Tenement Museum**, 90 Orchard St, between Broome and Delancey (Tuesday to Friday 12 noon–5pm, weekends from 11am; suggested admission $8). Centered around a restored six-story tenement that dates to 1870, it includes a gallery with slide shows and changing exhibits, as well as multi-ethnic neighborhood walking tours on weekends. (For information, call 431 0233.)

Co-existing with the old, historically Jewish Lower East Side are signs of a new downtown energy, seen in the alternative bars, clubs and boutiques springing up on Ludlow Street, which runs parallel to Orchard. From either, it's a relatively short hike up to the **East Village**, home of alternative lifestylers since Alan Ginsberg, Abbie Hoffman and the Hell's Angels set up shop in the 1960s. One of the easiest routes is to take a left on East Houston and a right onto the Bowery, a decrepit byway that evokes not entirely untruthful images of urban and human blight. Walk briskly past such semi-cultural landmarks as CBGB, the classic punk-rock club, until you reach East 4th Street. Turn left here, then take a right on Lafayette Street and continue uptown.

At the corner of Lafayette and 6th streets, the **Joseph Papp Public Theater** is headquartered in the majestic former **Astor Library**, built in the late 1800s. Across the street, another architectural highlight – **Colonnade Row** – hasn't fared as well, its white-marble facade now gray and crumbling.

Turn right at Astor Place, walk past the giant steel 'Alamo' cube, and crosss to St Mark's Place. The immense brownstone structure to your left is **Cooper Union**, established by Peter Cooper in 1859 as a college for the underprivileged. Abraham Lincoln made his critical 'Might Makes Right' speech here in 1860, a turning point in his bid for the presidency.

Continue across Cooper Square to St Mark's Place – Main Street, East Village – and one of the few places where the underground comes up for air. The overall motif here is radical chic, the grungier the better, with a healthy dash of left-wing politics. You will stumble across studs-and-leather rock shops, counter-culture bookstores and funky cafes where the anti-hip come to see and be seen. The scene gets rougher and the graffiti gets thicker as you approach **Tompkins Square Park**, once a sort of tent city for the homeless, but recently cleaned-up and restored.

Neighborhood mural

One block down Avenue A, turn right at 7th Street, and then return to Second Avenue. When you get to Second Avenue, turn right and walk up to 9th Street. You'll find there are enough restaurants in the next block to satisfy anyone's tastes. On the corner of 9th, for instance, **Veselka** will set you up with delicious and inexpensive Ukrainian food, not to mention the latest editions of Ukrainian newspapers. The **Second Avenue Delicatessen** serves up pastrami sandwiches as legendary as the Yiddish actors whose names grace the 'Walk of Fame' just outside the door. The atmosphere is just as frenetic, but in a much cooler way, at **Time Cafe**, a trendy restaurant-cum-basement jazz club, at 380 Lafayette Street across from the Public Theater.

If you've still got some energy to burn afterwards, wash down dinner with a couple of cold ones over at **McSorley's Old Ale House** on 7th Street near Third Avenue. Drinking here is an adventure in male-bonding. There's sawdust on the floor and suds on tap. Until the law was changed in 1970, not a woman was allowed in the house.

Orchard Street Market

A walking tour of shops and architecture followed by dinner and a nightclub.

At the geographical heart of Greenwich Village is **Washington Square Park**, and with its usual mix of students, drug peddlers, carriage-pushing mothers and the homeless, it is a showcase of the social incongruities that animate the neighborhood.

New York University dominates the square. Most of the newer and larger buildings that huddle around the edges are used for classrooms or administrative offices. Thankfully, NYU has seen fit to spare the

Characteristic town house

charming townhouses on **Washington Square North**, about the only 19th-century structures still facing the park with the exception of **Judson Memorial Church**, on the opposite side.

Start this walking ttour at Stanford White's **Washington Arch**, built in honor of the 100th anniversary of George Washington's inauguration. Walk a block up Fifth Avenue to 8th Street, pausing for a look at **Washington Mews**, a tidy enclave of rowhouses tucked into the middle of the block.

Turn left at 8th Street and walk over to Sixth Avenue. A few decades ago, **8th Street** was one of the hippest spots in the Village. These days, it's a haven for shoe-shoppers, with half the block toward Sixth crammed with stores devoted to shoes of all shapes, sizes and styles, often at prices that are half those asked in uptown stores. There are also some interesting boutiques, heavy on leather and chains.

When you come to the intersection of 8th Street and Sixth Avenue (also known as Village Square), get a good long look at the **Jefferson Market Courthouse**, a fairy-tale castle complete with everything but a moat and a maiden in distress. Completed in 1877, this Victorian beauty originally served as a courthouse and prison. Local devotees saved it from the wrecking ball in the late 1960s, and these days it's a branch of the **public library**.

Balducci's gourmet shop is just across the way, at the corner of 9th Street and Sixth. As far as Villagers are concerned, it's the last word in designer foods. The

Washington Square arch

Bust buy

people at Zabar's uptown may not agree, but take a look around and judge for yourself. The glorious smells alone make a visit worthwhile.

From the corner of 9th Street, walk straight across Village Square for a quick peek through the windows of antique shops and galleries on Greenwich Avenue. There's a neat installment of **Pottery Barn** just a few doors away. Nearby, **Common Ground** carries colorful American Indian jewelry, while a little farther down, there is another shop specializing in Mexican pottery, tiles and handcrafted furniture.

Spend as much time as you like browsing in these and other shops, then drop in for a cappuccino at the **Peacock Caffe** (24 Greenwich Ave), a Village institution since the 1940s. Once you've revived, cross Greenwich Avenue and bear left back to Village Square and the start of **Christopher Street**, on your right. One of the gay community's main drags, it's lined by a number of small, interesting stores, including the **Oscar Wilde Memorial Bookshop** (15 Christopher St).

Follow Christopher across Seventh Avenue South, then turn left at **Bedford Street** into one of the quiet residential areas scattered throughout the neighborhood. The hole-in-the-wall bar at the corner of Morton Street is **Chumley's**, an old speakeasy and a favorite with Village literati and college kids.

When you hit Seventh Avenue again, bear right and walk one block to the lovely old townhouses at **St Luke's Place**. These are among the most desirable homes in the city. Jimmy Walker, the high-living Jazz Age mayor, resided at number 6.

Now walk around the bend and then turn right onto Hudson Street. Keep walking north from here and you'll soon discover the austere red brick mass of **St Luke's in the Fields** crouching near Grove Street. St Luke's was built in 1822, making it the third oldest church in the city.

Up still farther, the **White Horse Tavern** – which was one of Dylan

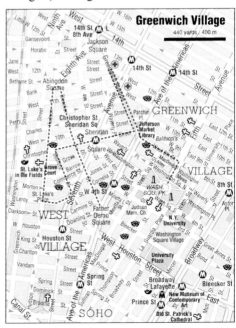

63

Shooting the breeze in a downtown cafe

Thomas's favorite haunts — stands amid a whole cluster of interesting antique stores and restaurants.

Past 11th Street, Hudson crosses a six-way intersection known as Abingdon Square. Turn more or less to your right and pick up **Bleecker Street** for a final pass through prime Village shopping.

Here most stores deal in antiques and traditional arts, although one happy exception — the **Biography Bookshop** — is located at the corner of 11th Street. A few doors down from here, **Susan Parrish** carries an inspired selection of antique quilts, furnishings and American folk art.

The shopping continues with even more variety down by **Charles Street**. **Pierre Deux** is a classy little place filled with fine French antiques while **Eastern Arts** carries exotic Asian pieces. Wrap up your shopping still farther down Bleecker at **Dorothy's Closet**, vintage clothiers *par excellence*, which has more sexy numbers than a Vegas revue.

As luck would have it, you're perfectly positioned for dinner. The stretch of Bleecker between Sixth and Seventh avenues is packed with Italian delis, pastry shops and at least two terrific restaurants. **Cucina Stagionale** (275 Bleecker St, near Jones St) is not only pretty as a picture, it serves an enticing choice of Italian dishes too good, and too inexpensive, to miss. Unfortunately, no one else in New York wants to miss them either — there's usually a line at the door by 7pm. If, on the other hand, you can't wait, duck over to **Tutta Pasta** (26 Carmine Street) instead. The room is cute, the prices are low, and the pasta is out of this world.

If Italian isn't in your stars tonight, you might consider **Cowgirl Hall of Fame** (519 Hudson St), a popular spot for barbecued ribs, chicken-fried steak and OK-Corral atmosphere. Or hop over to **Sweet Basil** (88 Seventh Avenue South) for a hot meal accompanied by a late-night set of cool jazz. Farther up, the **Village Vanguard** (178 Seventh Avenue South) is a tiny, smoky basement room where some of the world's great jazz musicians got their start and still perform.

12. SoHo Saturday

A tour of shops, galleries and cast-iron architecture followed by a meal at a local restaurant.

To put it simply, **SoHo** is one of the best ride in town. This old industrial neighborhood was invaded by artists in the 1960s and has since blossomed into a Mecca of avant-garde culture and bourgeois life. Between the galleries, boutiques and magnificent cast-iron architecture, there's enough to see and do here for a week,

much less a single afternoon or morning. This route leads you through some of the hot spots, but feel free to wander off whenever the urge strikes you. Take your time, indulge yourself, and enjoy SoHo for what it is – a playground for the rich and artsy. Plan to visit on Saturday, when gallery-hopping is at its best and street life is in full swing.

Kick off your tour at the top of West Broadway, where it meets West Houston Street. Walk south toward Canal Street: there are enough shops,

Have your portrait painted

restaurants and galleries along the way to keep you occupied for an entire weekend – including **Leo Castelli** (420 W. Broadway), which specializes in trend-setting contemporary art. Check out the lingerie at **Joovay** (436), the super-slick housewares at **Ad Hoc** (410) and the plastic oddities at **Hotel Venus** by **Patricia Field**, where even the cosmetics come in neon shades.

Turn right onto Prince Street for **Untitled Fine Art in Print**,

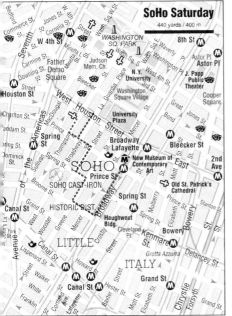

which indexes its postcard library alphabetically. If you're in the mood for outrageous women's wear, take another quick right on Thompson Street to **Betsey Johnson**.

Returning to West Broadway, cross to the other side of **Prince Street** for some serious browsing at both **No Name** (French shoes) and **Agnes B.** (French ready-to-wear). Or take a right on Wooster Street and walk a block down to **Spring Street**, where a

small open-air market at the corner of Spring and Wooster sells an eclectic mix of jewelry, clothes and shoulder bags. The next street up is **Greene Street;** turn right here for a look at the heart of SoHo's **Cast-Iron District.** The two standouts here are **numbers 28–30** (between Canal and Grand) and **72–76** (between Broome and Spring), hinting at Italian *palazzi* rendered in glorious detail. Like other cast-iron structures on Greene, these were built in the late 1800s as SoHo's fling with high society was coming to an end. Manufacturers moved into the area and threw up the prefabricated frames for warehouses and factories. The cast-iron technique was not only cheap and quick, but aesthetically pleasing. Iron could be cast into any shape, allowing for all sorts of architectural flourishes previously limited to stone.

In addition to striking architecture there are several galleries and art cooperatives to explore here, including **M-13** (72 Greene) and the **Heller Gallery** (71 Greene). Turn left on Broome Street and left again on **lower Broadway**, where the **Haughwout Building** on the far corner is another of the area's oldest (1857) and most striking cast-iron edifices. Back toward Prince Street, the **'Little Singer' Building** (561 Broadway) is yet another masterwork. In its own way, so is **Dean & DeLuca** across the street: a gourmet food store where every display is a work of art.

A gourmet heaven

Broadway is literally packed with galleries: from **560** (next door to D & D) to **568** alone there are nearly 50. Check the listings in *New York* magazine or pick up a copy of the *Gallery Guide*, a free publication available at just about any gallery. There are also five worthwhile museums in the immediate vicinity: the **Guggenheim Museum Soho** at 575 Broadway; the **New Museum of Contemporary Art** (583); the **Museum for African Art** (593); the **Children's Museum of the Arts**, a hands-on experience for kids; and the artists-founded **Alternative Museum** (594), which presents exhibits with a social or political slant.

As far as food is concerned, Soho is brimming over with possibilities. If you stumble on an irresistible bistro, help yourself. Otherwise, recommended local eateries range from casual places like the **Cupping Room Cafe** (359 W. Broadway), **Fanelli** (94 Prince St) and **Jerry's** (101 Prince St), to the posher ambience of **Raoul's** (180 Prince St) and the **Canal House Restaurant** at the Soho Grand Hotel (310 W. Broadway).

If the city is getting on your nerves, think about taking a 'sanity trip' to **The Cloisters** in **Washington Heights**. The Cloisters (Tuesday to Sunday 9.30am–4.45 or 5.15pm) is a branch of the Met specializing in medieval art and architecture. The exhibits are integrated into the building, much of it reconstructed from bits of 12th-century monasteries and churches. The result is an enchanting composite of old and new designed to recreate the hushed atmosphere of a medieval cloister. It's serene, meditative, frequently astonishing, and as far away from Manhattan as you can get without actually leaving the island.

Because the museum is set apart from the neighborhood, it's best if you lunch near your hotel before setting off. Then, if money is no object, hop a cab uptown. Alternatively you can take the IND Eighth Avenue A train through Harlem to 190th Street. Take the elevator to street level, and then follow Margaret Corbin Drive five blocks north to **Fort Tyron Park**. If you're leaving from the east side, catch the M-4 bus from Madison Avenue. The ride is longer, but you're dropped off at the the Cloisters' front door (the last stop).

The Cloisters, built by John D. Rockefeller Jr on behalf of the Metropolitan Museum of Art, rises like a medieval castle from a hilltop overlooking the Hudson River. The main body of the collection was assembled by George Grey Bernard, an American sculptor who recovered his treasures from church ruins, villages, even barnyards. The museum opened in 1938 and has one of the finest collections of medieval art in the world.

The central installment of the museum is the **Cuxa Cloister**, taken from a 12th-century French Benedictine monastery. Its arcade surrounds a medieval herb garden, and features Romanesque capitals, many adorned with grotesque beasts and monkeys. Madrigals play discreetly from hidden speakers, and in the summer, musicians in period costumes occasionally wander about.

Mostly laid out around the Cuxa Cloister in roughly chronolog-

The Cloisters: a piece of medieval Europe in Washington Heights

ical order, it starts at the main entrance with the simple grandeur of the **Romanesque Hall**, incorporating monumentals portals from 12th- and 13th-century Spain and France, and then branches into two large chapels featuring 12th-century frescoes, a magnificent carved altar canopy and a rare *Madonna and Child* carved in wood.

The *Unicorn Tapestries*, probably the museum's most famous possessions, hang nearby, playing out a complex allegory of courtly love and Christian mystery through the highly detailed and animated rendering of the unicorn's capture. You step down into the **Gothic Chapel**, built around the tomb effigies of Spanish nobility and a crusade knight, depicted in full armor, his hands joined in prayer.

Two more outdoor cloisters lead off the lower level and offer magnificent views over the New Jersey palisades across the Hudson River. Rockefeller found the sight so stirring, he bought land on the opposite bank so the view would never be spoiled.

The **Treasury** is also on this level with smaller and more delicate pieces

Stained-glass detail

such as liturgical fans encrusted with gems, ornate reliquaries, chalices, and carved oak paneling. The most exceptional works on display include a beautiful *Book of Hours* used by monks for their daily prayer recitation, and a single 16th-century rosary bead carved in fine detail.

The museum generally closes at 5.15pm (earlier in winter), and the suggested admission is $8 for adults, $4 for students and seniors. If you want to postpone your return to reality, you can't do better than dine at the **Terrace** (400 W. 119th St), an elegant eatery high atop Columbia University's Butler Hall, between Morningside Drive and Amsterdam Avenue. The view from here is spectacular, the Mediterranean-style cuisine is first-rate, and it's well worth splurging on a taxi ride to get there in comfort. Dinner service doesn't start until 6pm, giving you ample time to go back to your hotel and dress up. The Terrace is open for lunch, too; call 666-9490 to make reservations.

Romanesque doorway

Two of the zoo's 4,000 inmates

14. The Bronx Zoo / Wildlife Conservation Park

One of the country's oldest urban zoos, the 265-acre (107-hectare) **Bronx Zoo/Wildlife Conservation Park** opened in 1899. While its focus may have changed from mainly exhibitions to education and conservation, it's still New York's largest zoo, where you can find over 4,000 animals, including many rare and/or endangered species. For most of the year, the animals are kept in simulated habitats, including a large wilderness area in which Asian elephants, antelope, tigers and rhinoceroses roam about while visitors watch from an elevated monorail. There are also impressive recreations of tropical rainforests and Himalayan highlands as well as a reptile house, aviary and children's zoo.

The best time to visit is from April to October, since some of the animals are unable to withstand the cold winter months, and a few attractions – like the monorail – are closed then. The zoo is open from 10am to 5pm Monday through Friday, and until 5.30pm on Saturday and Sunday. From November to March, admission is $3 for adults and $1.50 for kids; from April to October, $6.75 and $3 (free Weds). Children under two are admitted free all year round.

The **New York Botanical Garden** is located across Fordham Road from the zoo's main Rainey Gate entrance. If you have any interest in botany, or just enjoy looking at beautiful plants, this is a fascinating and peaceful place to while away a few hours. If you plan on visiting the zoo anyway, it's well worth allocating a little extra time for the gardens. (For hours and fees call 718-817-8700).

The quickest way to the zoo from Manhattan is by subway. Take the IRT Seventh Ave, **#2 Express** to the **Pelham Parkway Station** or take the IRT Lexington Ave. **#5 train** to the **East 180th St. Station** and then transfer to the #2 to Pelham Parkway Station. You can also catch a Metro North train from Grand Central Terminal to the Fordham Station, then pick up a Bx9 bus to the zoo's Southern Boulevard entrance. Call 718-367-1010 for more information.

Shopping

Shopping in Manhattan could easily become a full-time occupation. From *haute couture* to bargain basement, Stone-Age art to high technology, the city is one big marketplace. As they say, if something exists, it exists in New York, and if you've got enough money, it can probably be bought.

Like everything else in the city, shopping changes dramatically from one neighborhood to another. In **Midtown**, you'll find large department stores catering to the middle and upper classes. **Fifth Avenue, 57th Street** and **Madison Avenue** are crowded with chichi stores for the ultra-fashionable. The **Upper West Side**, principally Columbus Avenue, is known for smaller specialty boutiques that are usually less expensive and more daring than their haughty counterparts on the **Upper East Side**. Downtown, the shops get a bit funkier. **SoHo** is a good place for cutting-edge style; **Greenwich Village** is one of the best places for antiques; lower Broadway offers high-end clothes and furnishings; the **East Village** and the **Lower East Side** represents alternative chic.

Fashion

Keeping up with the latest fashion is a never-ending mission. In addition to the areas already mentioned, give upper Madison Avenue a try: there's a wild selection of pricey cowboy duds at **Billy Martin's**, on the corner of 68th Street; the latest in breakthrough Japanese-wear at **Kenzo**, a block farther up; and the elegant **Polo/Ralph Lauren** takes up an entire mansion at the corner of 72nd.

In midtown, you can't do better than **Brooks Brothers** (346 Madison Avenue), famous for its classic Ivy-League duds. On the Upper West Side and other locales throughout the city, **Charivari** (58 West 72nd St) offers styles that are casual, expensive and definitely cool. In the East Village area, **Trash and Vaudeville** (4 St Mark's

Bloomingdale's has it all

The Canal Jeans Co. in Broadway

Place) is a boutique with an edgy, radical attitude; and **Canal Jeans Co**. (504 Broadway) is a hangar-sized operation for reasonably priced new jeans, old army coats, etc. In SoHo, the possibilities range from the high-fashion Japanese wear at **Commes des Garçons** (116 Wooster St) to the vintage Victorian dresses and nightgowns at **Harriet Love** (126 Prince St) to the colorful ethnic gear at **Putumayo** (147 Spring St).

Books and Music

As a major center for both the publishing and recording industries, New York has one of the widest selections of retail outlets in the world. Besides book chains like **Barnes & Noble**, **Brentano's** and **Borders Books and Music**, or local music chains like **Sam Goody** (located throughout Manhattan), there are numerous independents, including **Forbidden Planet** (821 Broadway; tel: 473-1576) for sci-fi and fantasy; **Murder Ink** (2486 Broadway; tel: 362-8905) for mystery and crime; and **St Mark's Bookshop** (31 Third Avenue; tel: 260-7853), an East Village shop specializing in alternative themes; and the Strand Book Store (828 Broadway, tel: 473-1452), which advertises eight miles of old, new and rare books.

You can find books about New York City at **New York Bound** (50 Rockefeller Plaza; tel: 245-8503); books about everywhere at **The Complete Traveller** (199 Madison Avenue; tel: 685-9007) and the **Traveller's Bookstore** (22 West 52nd St; tel: 664-0995); and some of the biggest-volume selections at **Coliseum Books** (1771 Broadway at 57th St; tel: 757-8381) and **Tower Books** (383 Lafayette St; tel: 228-5100).

For a mind-boggling variety of CDs and tapes, try **Tower Records** (692 Broadway; tel: 505-1500) or HMV (Lexington Avenue at 86th St; tel: 348-0800 and Broadway at 72nd St; tel: 721-5900; and 565 Fifth Avenue, tel: 681-6700). **J & R Music World** (23 Park Row; tel: 238-9000) has an excellent jazz and classical section, while both **House of Oldies** (35 Carmine St; tel: 243-0500) and **Bleecker Bob's** (118 W. 3rd St; tel: 475-9677) offer rare vinyl classics.

Electronics

The city also has some great offers in cameras, computers and other electronics. An important caveat: be sure you know exactly what you're buying. Most discount stores make their money on volume, not service. Take the salesman's pitch with a grain of salt, and don't be afraid to make an offer they can't refuse (though they may, loudly).

Convince yourself

In addition to chain stores like **Radio Shack** and the **Wiz**, good places to start looking include: **47th Street Photo** (115 W. 45th St; closed Saturdays) for discounts on almost everything electronic, including laptop computers; **The Fone Booth** (330 Seventh Avenue) for upscale answering machines and cordless phones; and **Camera Land** (575 Lexington Avenue, between 51st and 52nd streets) or **Willoughby's** (136 W. 32nd St), for anything to do with cameras, including rentals and servicing.

Gourmet Shops

The designer food business in Manhattan is dominated by the gourmet trinity: **Zabar's** (2245 Broadway, near 80th St), **Balducci's** (424 Sixth Avenue, near 9th St), and **Dean & DeLuca** (560 Broadway). The best place for ethnic goodies is in the appropriate neighborhoods. **Mott** and **Mulberry streets** are lined with vegetable stands, fishmongers, cheese shops and delis in both **Chinatown** and **Little Italy**. **East Houston** and **Essex Street** are the places to go for Jewish delicacies in the Lower East Side. There is still a scattering of German and Hungarian places in **Yorkville**, and **La Marqueta**, on Park Avenue between 111th and 116th streets in **East Harlem**, is an open-air market frequented by the local Hispanic community.

Bargains

Your greatest assets as a bargain-shopper are time, patience and *chutzpah*. Determined deal-makers can dig up some terrific buys, if they know where to look. For clothes and fabrics, the **Lower East Side** is discount central. The action is around **Orchard Street**, where it pays to haggle. Thrift shops and flea markets are also good places to try. There are several thrift stores on **Third Avenue** between 81st and 92nd streets, and small flea markets are held at the corner of **Broadway** and **East 4th Street (East Village)**, the corner of **Spring** and **Wooster (SoHo)**, and on **Columbus Avenue** between **76th** and **77th streets**. The most eclectic is held on weekends along **Sixth Avenue** between **25th** and **27th streets**, where hip New Yorkers go to be seen.

Bargain-hunting on Columbus

Eating Out

Eating out is a quintessential part of the New York experience. The incredible variety and quality of the city's restaurants make New York one of the gourmet capitals of the world. No doubt about it, food is one of New York's great pleasures, but there's more to it than just putting something tasty in your mouth. After all, meals are social events. They're part of the tone and rhythm of everyday life, and as such they provide a great opportunity to experience local culture. Whether it's a noodle shop in Chinatown, a yuppie hang-out on the Upper West Side or a four-star dining room on Fifth Avenue, New York restaurants are a great place to go to rub elbows with native New Yorkers.

First, and most obviously, you're going to need money. Depending on your tastes, eating in Manhattan can be very expensive. In the finer restaurants, for example, you can expect to spend at least $70 or $80 a head. Even in the so-called moderate range, it's not difficult to rack up a bill of $30 or $40 each. If you plan on doing New York on a budget, however, there's no reason to panic. There are still plenty of places where you can find wholesome, filling meals for as little as $20. Chinatown, Little Italy and the Lower East Side are the most reliable neighborhoods for cheap eats, but you can also try the Indian restaurants on East 6th Street, the hearty German and Hungarian fare in Yorkville and coffeehouses just about everywhere. In general, lunch tends to be less expensive than dinner, and in midtown at least, pre-theater specials help put even upscale places within reach of most visitors' budgets.

The other thing you need to remember about eating in Manhattan is that reservations are absolutely essential. Unless you plan on eating at a diner or cafeteria, be sure to call ahead. If you plan on going to one of the hot new eateries everybody's raving about, you should probably call several days, if not weeks, in advance. And

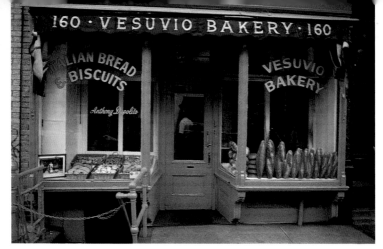

Bread like mama used to bake

even if you have reservations, don't be surprised if you have to wait a while to be seated. (A tip to the maître d' may speed the wait, or it may not.) In the end, the only surefire way of beating the crowds is to eat at off-hours.

Finally, the key to eating out in Manhattan is a healthy sense of adventure. If meat-and-potatoes represent the breadth of your culinary experience, you may be in for a shock. Whether it's unusual ethnic cuisine (had any Ethiopian lately?), odd-ball combinations (Cuban-Chinese, Indian-Mexican, Jewish-Italian), old classics (hotdog and pretzel), or cutting edge, Manhattan is the place to let your gastronomic imagination run wild.

For the sake of rounding out the selection offered in the itineraries, here are a few more restaurants to keep in mind. Most are moderately priced, and several offer Sunday brunch, a beloved New York tradition.

Downtown

ARQUA
281 Church St
Tel: 334-1888
Chic Tuscan restaurant that packs them in down in TriBeCa. The food is exquisite. On the pricey side but worth it.

BENNY'S BURRITOS
113 Greenwich Avenue
Tel: 727-0584
First-class cheap eats in the West Village. Get a couple of Benny's overstuffed *burritos* in your belly and you'll feel you don't need to eat for a week.

DOJO
24 St Mark's Place
Tel: 674-9821
Japanese-California health food with a distinctly East Village edge. Sit on the patio and watch the parade on St Mark's Place. Extremely affordable.

INDOCHINE
430 Lafayette
Tel: 505-5111
Upscale Vietnamese restaurant that's a favorite of the East Village-SoHo crowd.

MIRACLE GRILL
112 First Avenue
Tel: 254-2353
A little piece of Santa Fe in the East Village with interesting southwestern-influenced dishes and a neat patio out back.

Cafe conversation

MITALI
334 E. 6th St
Tel: 533-2508
Delicious Indian food at affordable prices. Probably the best of the 6th Street Indian places in the East Village.

ODEON
145 W. Broadway
Tel: 233-0507
This is the classic TriBeCa eatery. The clientele is cool, the prices are pretty reasonable. Best after midnight, when serious partiers come out to play. Check it out for Sunday brunch, too.

PUGLIA
189 Hester St
Tel: 226-8912
Noisy, boisterous, sociable and cheap. Everybody eats at common tables and talks at the same time. Not the place for a romantic evening, but a great belly-filler that captures the excitable atmosphere of Little Italy better than most.

Pizza: a fast food favorite

SAMMY'S ROUMANIAN STEAK HOUSE
157 Chrystie St
Tel: 673-0330
Jewish restaurant on the Lower East Side. The food is good and hearty, but heavy on the schtick – and the music is numbingly loud.

WINDOWS ON THE WORLD
1 World Trade Center
Tel: 524-7000
It's expensive – but considering the fantastic 107th-floor view, you'd expect it to be. The restaurant offers an only-in-New York experience; open for dinner nightly and brunch on weekends.

Midtown

AKBAR
475 Park Avenue
Tel: 838-1717
Very good Indian cuisine. Considering the ritzy location, the price of the *prix-fixe* lunch here is rock bottom.

BRYANT PARK CAFE
25 W. 40th St
Tel: 840-6500
Overlooking Bryant Park, behind the Public Library at 42nd Street, serving good, reasonably priced American-style cuisine.

FOUR SEASONS
99 E. 52nd St
Tel: 754-9494
A high-profile Manhattan favorite, where the menu changes to reflect the seasons and the clientele includes movers and shakers from the business and publishing worlds. Very expensive.

JEZEBEL
630 Ninth Avenue
Tel: 582-1045
Southern-style American cooking served beneath fringed lamps and hanging antique lace dresses; on the expensive side, but great atmosphere.

THE MANHATTAN CHILI CO.
1500 Broadway (at 43rd St)
Tel: 730-8666
Pleasant, inexpensive place with 10 varieties of award-winning chili on offer. There's a *prix-fixe* dinner and a children's menu available, too.

LUTECE
249 E. 50th St
Tel: 752-2225
One of the best – maybe the best – French restaurant in New York. High-class but not too snooty. Prices are just short of astronomical.

PALM
837 Second Avenue
Tel: 687-2953
Come with an appetite, because the portions are huge. A boisterous steak and lobster place with plenty of atmosphere. All this good food doesn't come cheap. You should count on around $50 a head.

Sweet sensations

P.J. CLARKE'S
915 Third Avenue
Tel: 759-1650
A classic New York watering-hole. One of the best places in the city to come for a beer, a friendly chat and a juicy burger.

TIBETAN KITCHEN
444 Third Avenue
Tel: 679-6286
Solid vegetarian dishes from the land of the Dalai Lama.

ZARELA
953 Second Avenue
Tel: 644-6740
Reasonably-priced, home-cooked Mexican food in a lively setting.

UNION SQUARE CAFE
21 East 16th St
Tel: 243-4020
Closer to downtown than midtown, in the increasingly fashionable blocks around Union Square. Innovative nouvelle-American cuisine attracts a stylish crowd. One of the city's best.

Uptown

ELIO'S
1621 Second Avenue
Tel: 772-2242
Fairly expensive Northern Italian eatery frequented by a well-dressed clientele.

FUJIYAMA MAMA
467 Columbus Avenue (at 82nd St)
Tel: 769-1144
Techno-sushi. New-wave Japanese served up with plenty of rock and roll. Fun but expensive.

LA CARIDAD
2199 Broadway (at 78th St)
Upper West Side
Tel: 874-2780
Solid Cuban-Chinese plate. Good food at rock bottom prices.

LA COTE BASQUE
0 W. 55th St
Tel: 688-6525
Fine dining in an elegant atmosphere. One of the city's best, and oldest, French restaurants.

MUGHLAI
20 Columbus Avenue (at 75th St)
Tel: 724-6363
Good Indian food at reasonable, but not cheap, prices.

MUSEUM CAFE
366 Columbus Avenue (at 77th)
Tel: 799-0150
An original yuppie hang-out, and still a reliable spot for basic, no-frills entrees. A short walk from the Museum of Natural History.

And for dessert...

RATHBONES
1702 Second Avenue
Tel: 369-7361
Offers good steaks, burgers and beers for under 20 bucks per head in an inviting pub atmosphere. Star-gazers can watch the limousines pull up outside Elaine's (*see below*), located just across the street.

ELAINE'S
1703 Second Avenue
Tel: 534-8103
Remains one of the Uptown places where the elite meet to eat, but unless you have been invited here by one of its regulars, you may want to pass it up.

SAN DOMENICO
240 Central Park South
Tel: 265-5959
This is one of the most highly rated Italian restaurants in the city, with an exceptional variety of dishes all wonderfully cooked. It offers an extremely large wine list, too. Rather formal, and expensive – unless you go *prix fixe*.

SERENDIPITY 3
225 E. 60th St
Tel: 838-3531
Strange, fanciful, one-of-a-kind. Give yourself a little extra time just to check out the outrageous kitsch. Entrées are basic kids' stuff and desserts are monstrous. A great way to cap off an evening on the town. You may spy a celeb, too.

SIGN OF THE DOVE
1110 Third Avenue
Tel: 861-8080
A beautiful and gracious setting for carefully prepared cuisine. Proper attire is essential here. You should expect to spend at least $60 per person for dinner.

Nightlife

The two things for a successful night on the town are reservations and money. Popular Broadway shows, concerts, even nightclub acts, are often booked weeks in advance. It pays to call well ahead of time.

As far as money goes, expect to spend a lot. To give you a rough idea, Broadway tickets can be

TKTS for half-price tickets

$75 the best seats, good seats at the Metropolitan Opera go somewhere between $50 and $100, and after you tally up the cover charge and drink minimum at nightclubs you are usually well over $25 a head.

Most of the time it's worth it. New York City attracts the best and brightest talent in the entire country.

Your best sources of information are the *New York Times, New York Magazine, The New Yorker* and *Time Out*. Useful numbers for information about theater, dance and music events include NYC/ON STAGE, tel: 768-1818; and the Broadway Line, tel: 563-2929.

Theater

Theater falls into three categories: Broadway, off-Broadway, and off-off-Broadway. Generally, Broadway has the slickest and most expensive productions. Off-Broadway offers high-quality productions for less money. And off-off-Broadway often presents experimental works for not much more than the price of a movie.

Broadway

Same-day, half-price tickets are available at two TKTS locations for shows not already sold out. Cash-only sales; although traveler's checks are accepted.

TKTS
47th Street and Broadway
Tel: 768-1818
Monday to Saturday from 3–8pm for evening performances. Saturday and Wednesday from 10–2pm for matinees. Sunday from noon to closing for matinees and evenings.

TKTS
Two World Trade Center
Mezzanine level

Monday–Friday 11am–5.30pm for evening performances, and Saturday 11am–3.30pm for Sunday matinee and evening shows.

Off-Broadway Theaters

CHERRY LANE THEATER
38 Commerce St
Tel: 989-2020

DOUGLAS FAIRBANKS THEATER
432 W. 42nd St
Tel: 239-4321

IRISH REPERTORY THEATER
132 W. 22nd St
Tel: 727-2737

LUCILLE LORTEL THEATER
121 Christopher St
Tel: 924-8782

MANHATTAN THEATER CLUB
131 W. 55th St
Tel: 581-1212

MINETTA LANE THEATRE
18 Minetta Lane
Tel: 420-8000

ORPHEUM THEATER
126 Second Avenue
Tel: 477-2477

PEARL THEATER COMPANY
80 St Mark's Place
Tel: 598-9802

JOSEPH PAPP PUBLIC THEATER
425 Lafayette St
Tel: 260-2400

PLAYWRIGHT'S HORIZON
416 W. 42nd St
Tel: 279-4200

SHAKESPEARE IN THE PARK
Delacorte Theater, Central Park
Tel: 539-8500
July and August. Open-air; free tickets on same day as performance. Always long lines.

Off-Off-Broadway Theaters

LA MAMA E.T.C.
74a E. 4th St
Tel: 475-7710

ONTOLOGICAL-HYSTERIC THEATER
260 W. Broadway
Tel: 941-8911

P.S. 122
150 First Avenue
(at 9th Street)
Tel: 477-5288

Old Provincetown Playhouse on MacDougal Street

SOHO REPERTORY THEATER
46 Walker St
Tel: 334-0962

THEATER FOR THE NEW CITY
155 First Avenue
Tel: 475-0108

Opera lovers love the Met

THE YORK THEATER COMPANY
St Peter's Church
Lexington and 54th St
Tel: 935-5820

Music, Dance, Opera

ALICE TULLY HALL
Lincoln Center
Tel: 875-5050
Julliard's theater for 'small' performances. Great for chamber music.

AVERY FISHER HALL
Lincoln Center
Tel: 875-5030
Kurt Masur conducts the New York Philharmonic, September to May. The popular Mostly Mozart series takes place here, July and August.

BROOKLYN ACADEMY OF MUSIC (BAM)
30 Lafayette Avenue, Brooklyn
Tel: 718-636-4100
The annual Next Wave Festival, one of New York's premier avant-garde events, takes place here from October to December; other cutting edge pro-

ductions during the rest of the year.

CARNEGIE HALL
881 Seventh Avenue
Tel: 247-7800
Offers everything from classical to comedy in a landmark building.

CITY CENTER
131 W. 55th Street
Tel: 581-1212
Alvin Ailey, Joffrey Ballet, Dance Theater of Harlem perform here, as do various musical groups.

THE JOYCE THEATER
175 Eighth Avenue
Tel: 242-0800
Performances by innovative dance troupes make this one of the most exciting venues in town.

METROPOLITAN OPERA HOUSE
Lincoln Center
Tel: 362-6000
The American Ballet Theater performs here from April to June; the Metropolitan opera from October to April. Standing room tickets are occasionally available before the performance at a fraction of the regular price. Call for details.

NEW YORK STATE THEATER
Lincoln Center
Tel: 870-5570
The NYC Ballet dances here: so does The New York City Opera (*The Nutcracker* is a special Christmas treat). The New York City Opera performs September to November and again starting in March.

TOWN HALL
123 West 43rd St
Tel: 840-2824
Jazz and other musical events held in this Moorish-style building throughout the year.

Nightclubs

New York's club scene has slowed down slightly in recent years, but it is still one of the most varied in the world. At some clubs the bouncers only admit the customers they consider cool enough — waiting for their verdict is traditionally one of the city's most humiliating rituals.

For even a fairly modest night on the town, you will need plenty of money. To avoid unhappy surprises, call ahead to check on cover charge and minimum drink charges.

Jazz

BLUE NOTE
131 W. 3rd St, near Sixth Avenue
Tel: 475-8592
A jazz classic. A little on the pricey side, but some of the world's top performers make it worthwhile.

IRIDIUM
44 W. 63rd St
Tel: 582-2121
Since opening in 1994 this club near Lincoln Center has presented some of the jazz world's most gifted denizens.

SWEET BASIL
88 Seventh Ave South, at Bleecker St
Tel: 242-1785

A restaurant and jazz club that's a Village classic, popular for weekend brunches.

VILLAGE VANGUARD
178 Seventh Avenue South
Tel: 255-4037
Over 60 years old and still bringing in the biggies.

Rock, Blues and Country

THE BOTTOM LINE
15 W. 4th St.
Tel: 228-6300
Come here for the best folk-rock acts in town.

CBGB
315 Bowery
Tel: 982-4052
This is an old Downtown standby presenting a new generation of hardcore rockers.

MANNY'S CAR WASH
1558 Third Avenue
Tel: 369-2583
This is a rambling Upper East Side bar and club devoted to Chicago-style blues.

MERCURY LOUNGE
217 E. Houston St
Tel: 260-4700

Late-night line-up

One of Downtown's most popular venues for top alternative bands and performers.

PADDY REILLY'S MUSIC BAR
519 Second Avenue
Tel: 686-1210
Not much to look at, but plenty of Guinness on tap, along with performances by Irish bands some nights.

TRAMPS
45 West 21st St
Tel: 727-7788
A good-time Chelsea music club with a bayou flair, featuring Cajun, zydeco, rock and Southern-fried boogie.

WETLANDS
161 Hudson St
Tel: 966-5244
Live music and good vibes, *nouveau* Sixties style. Retro, but fun.

Dancing, Drinking and Cabaret

CHINA CLUB
2130 Broadway
Tel: 877-1166
This is an established Upper West Side dance club with a bar, cocktail lounge and, on some evenings, live bands.

DELIA'S
197 E. 3rd St
Tel: 254-9184
A tiny, classy East Village venue for dining and dancing.

IRVING PLAZA
17 Irving Place
Tel: 777-6800
A dilapidated hall near Gramercy Park

The temperature rises

that's gone through several incarnations, currently featuring everything from jazz and alternative rock to ballroom dancing.

MARIE'S CRISIS
59 Grove St
Tel: 243-9323
A mostly gay bar with cabaret sing-alongs seven nights a week.

NELL'S
246 W. 14th St
Tel: 675-1567
An Eighties survivor still pulling in the crowds. Dress to impress – or the doormen may never let you in.

S.O.B.
204 Varick St, at Houston
Tel: 243-4940
The name of this restaurant/dance club stands for 'Sounds of Brazil,' but the repertoire includes everything from West African singers to salsa.

THE SUPPER CLUB
240 W. 47th St
Tel: 921-1940
A romantic throwback to the heyday of New York City nightclubs, with dining and dancing to '40s-style big bands and occasional appearances by top contemporary rock acts.

Comedy

CAROLINE'S
1626 Broadway
Tel: 757-4100
Lush, plush and features some of the city's hippest comics.

THE COMEDY CELLAR
117 MacDougal St
Tel: 254-3480
A cramped basement room where the tables are so close together you'll make new friends – even if you don't get the jokes.

PRACTICAL information

TRAVEL ESSENTIALS

When to Visit

The two best times are spring and fall, when temperatures are moderate and the seasons are changing. The Christmas season is also a great time to come, although December and January can be extremely cold and snowy. July, August and early September can be hot and humid, and many New Yorkers escape to the beach or mountains, especially on weekends. If you don't mind sweating, these months offer a great way of beating the crowds.

Visas and Customs

Most foreign travelers to the United States must have a passport, a visa and, depending on where they are coming from, a health record. Exceptions to this rule include Canadians, British subjects from Bermuda or Canada entering from the western hemisphere, Germans, Italians, the Dutch, Swiss, British, French, Japanese and certain government officials.

All foreign visitors must go through US Customs. If you drive into the country, you may have your car and baggage searched by customs officials. Keep the following restrictions in mind:
• There is no limit to the amount of money you can bring with you, but if it exceeds $10,000, you must fill out a report.
• Items for your own personal use may be brought in duty- and tax-free.
• Gifts less than $400 can be brought in duty- and tax-free. Anything over $400 is subject to duty charges and taxes, but the next $1,000 worth is subject to a duty of only 10 percent.

Forward planning

Money Matters

Foreign currency is not accepted in New York City, and currency exchanges are few and far between (it can be almost impossible to change money on Sunday). It's best to arrive with at least $100 in small bills. Foreign money can be exchanged at most large hotels, but the best rates are found at banks.

You can also exchange money at Thomas Cook Currency Services (511 Madison Avenue at 53rd Street, tel: 753-2595) and at 1590 Broadway (tel: 265 6049). Another possibility is Ruesch International (608 Fifth Avenue, tel: 977-2700).

The basic unit of US money is the dollar, which comprises 100 cents. There are four coins you are likely to come across: the penny (worth 1 cent), the nickel (5 cents), the dime (10 cents) and the quarter (25 cents).

There are seven common denominations of paper money. The denominations are $1, $5, $10, $20, $50 and $100.

The most convenient and safest way to carry large sums of money is with traveler's checks. The two most widely accepted are

American Express and Visa. Almost all stores, restaurants and hotels will accept them. Credit cards (American Express, Visa, MasterCard, Diner's Club, and Discover) are also widely accepted, but check with clerks and waiters before ordering or buying.

If you have an Automatic Teller Machine (ATM) card, you will find ATMs everywhere in Manhattan. Check with your bank for a list of ATMs that will accept your particular card in New York.

Clothing

Just about anything goes in Manhattan, from grungy to elegant. But if you plan on attending any performances or eating at fine restaurants, you should bring along something on the formal side: jacket and tie for men, classy slacks or dresses for women. Although a few restaurants require formal attire, you can usually get away with something casual if it is well put together.

Appropriate attire depends on the season. Prepare for bone-chilling cold in winter, steamy hot days in summer, and moderate temperatures in spring and fall. In any case, try to dress in layers so you can peel on or off as circumstances dictate. Buildings are invariably overheated in winter and air-conditioned to the point of frostbite during the summer months. It's a good idea to bring an umbrella and other raingear, too, especially during the spring when rain can be heavy.

Geography

Manhattan is usually broken down into three broad areas: Downtown, Midtown and Uptown. Roughly speaking, Downtown runs from the southern tip of Manhattan to 14th Street and contains the Financial District, Chinatown, Little Italy, TriBeCa (triangle below Canal), SoHo, the Lower East Side, the East Village and Greenwich Village. Midtown starts at 14th Street and goes up to about the bottom of Central Park at 59th Street. Midtown includes the Flatiron District (including Union Square), Garment District, the Theater District, Clinton (formerly Hell's Kitchen), Turtle Bay, Chelsea and Midtown East. Uptown starts at 59th Street and runs all the way up to the northern tip of Manhattan, taking in the Upper West Side, the Upper East Side, Central Park, Morningside Heights, Harlem, East Harlem, Washington Heights and Inwood.

Both midtown and uptown are crisscrossed by a street grid. Avenues travel north and south, the lower numbers to the east and the higher numbers to the west. Streets travel east and west, the higher numbers to the north and the lower numbers to the south.

Fifth Avenue runs down the center of Manhattan. All the streets to the west of Fifth Avenue are preceded by the word 'West.' Port Authority Bus Terminal, for example, is on West 42nd Street. Similarly, all streets to the east of Fifth Avenue are preceded with the word 'East.' Grand Central Terminal is on East 42nd Street.

You will often hear New Yorkers refer to the east side or the west side of Manhattan, but never the north or the south. Instead, they use uptown and downtown as relative terms.

If you have a house number, but you're not sure exactly where it is, use this guide to pinpoint its location:

Street Numbers

Building numbers located between
East Side:
1–49	Fifth and Madison aves.
50–99	Madison and Park aves.
100–149	Park and Lexington aves.

View from the World Trade Center

150–199	Lexington and Third aves.
200–299	Third and Second aves.
300–399	Second and First aves.
400–499	First and York aves.

West Side:

1–99	Fifth and Sixth aves.
100–199	Sixth and Seventh aves.
200–299	Seventh and Eighth aves.
300–399	Eighth and Ninth aves.
400–499	Ninth and Tenth aves.
500–599	Tenth and Eleventh aves.
600–	Eleventh and Twelfth aves.

Avenue Numbers

In order to find the nearest crosss-street for an avenue address, strike the last number of the address, then divide by two and add or subtract the following numbers.

First Ave:	+3
Second Ave:	+3
Third Ave:	+10
Lexington Ave:	+22
Park Ave:	+34
Madison Ave:	+26
Fifth Ave:	
1–200	+13
201–400	+16
401–600	+18
601–775	+20
Sixth Ave:	–12
Seventh Ave:	
1–1800	+12
1801–	+20
Eighth Ave:	+9
Ninth Ave:	+13
Tenth Ave:	+14
Eleventh Ave:	+15
Broadway:	–30

Climate

New York has four distinct seasons: winter, spring, summer and fall. From late November to February you can expect temperatures anywhere from 40°F (5°C) to about 20°F (-6°C). From March to May temperatures range from 70°F (21°C) to about 35°F (2°C). From June to August temperatures range from about 90°F (32°C) to 60°F (15°C). And from September to early November temperatures range from 75°F (24°C) to 40°F (5°C). Snow is common in winter, and rain is common in spring.

Time

New York City runs on Eastern Standard Time. Every spring the clock is turned one hour ahead, and every fall one hour back. New York City is three hours ahead of Los Angeles, one hour ahead of Chicago, five hours behind London, and 15 hours behind Tokyo.

Safety

New York City has a reputation for crime, but in reality it's safer than many other North American cities. To stay safe, use commonsense. Don't carry large sums of money or wear flashy or expensive jewelry. Hang on to your purse or shoulder bag and keep your wallet in your front pocket. Women should avoid traveling alone late at night, and neither men or women should go into a strange or deserted area on their own. Your best asset is knowing where you are and where you're going. Walk purposefully, with confidence, even if you're lost.

If you need to take the subway at night be sure to stand near the token booth, a transit police officer or in the designated 'off-hour waiting areas.' Never ride in a car with just a few people in it. In general, buses and taxis are safer than the subway.

If you are mugged, walk or take a taxi to the nearest police station and report the crime. The police won't be much help finding your assailant, but they can do the proper paperwork for any insurance claims. There's no good response to a mugging. Your best bet is to give the mugger whatever he asks for and hope that's the end of it.

For police, medical or fire emergencies, call 911 anywhere in the city.

Tipping

As elsewhere, service personnel in New York City depend on tips for a large part of their income. In most cases, 15–20 percent is the going rate for waiters, taxi drivers, bartenders and barbers. Porters and bellman get about $0.75–1 for each bag, but never less than a dollar total.

Tourist Information

For brochures, maps, a calendar of events and hotel listings, contact or visit the New York Convention and Visitors Bureau (810 Seventh Avenue, New York, NY 10019, tel: 212-397-8200).

Tours

Organized tours fit just about any taste or interest. Some of the better tour operators (and tours) include:

Adventure on a Shoestring, 300 W. 53rd St, tel: 265-2663. Innovative weekend walking tours. Itineraries always changing. Call for the latest schedule.

Art Tours of New York, 682 Broadway, tel: 677-6005. For anyone interested in the New York gallery scene.

Backstage on Broadway, 228 W. 47th St, tel: 575-8065. Get a behind-the-scenes look at a Broadway production.

Gray Line Tours, 900 Eighth Avenue, tel: 397-2600. Bus and trolley tours; many itineraries.

Municipal Art Society, 457 Madison Avenue, tel: 935-3960. Architecture and landmarks around the city.

Museum of the City of New York, Fifth Avenue and 103rd St, tel: 534-1672. Sunday walking tours with an appropriately historical slant.

Urban Park Rangers, Central Park Arsenal, tel: 427-4040. Free nature walks in parks throughout the city.

Sports

New York has everything from tennis, skating and horseback riding in **Central Park** to the vast amenities of the new 30-acre **Chelsea Piers** complex (336-6666) along the Hudson River between W. 17th and W. 23rd Street, which includes a four-story golf driving range, two indoor skating rinks, a boat marina and a huge sports-fitness center with stunning river views (day passes available; call 336-6000). Major team sports are baseball May–October (Yankees at **Yankee Stadium**, tel: 718-293-6000); Mets at **Shea Stadium**, tel: 718-507-8499), basketball October–May (Knicks at **Madison Square Garden**, tel: 465-6741), football September–December (Jets and Giants at The **Meadowlands**, Rutherford, N.J., tel: 201-935-8500) and hockey October–April (Rangers at Madison Square Garden). U.S. Open tennis matches take place at the **USTA National Tennis Center**, Flushing Meadows, Corona Park, Queens, tel: 718-760-6200.

GETTING AROUND

Subways

Manhattan's subways can be intimidating, but they are the least expensive and quickest way to get around town. At press time, fares for all trains were $1.50. Tokens and Metro Cards (good for a minimum of two trips and accepted only at automated turnstiles) are bought at the glassed-in booths in most stations.

Generally speaking, Manhattan trains run uptown and downtown, and you can usually get where you're going on the IRT-Broadway Line's 1, 2 and 3 trains on the West Side; and on the IRT-Lexington Avenue Line's 4, 5 and 6 trains on the East Side. The two are connected at 42nd Street by the Grand Central-Times Square Shuttle (follow the 'S' signs) and at 14th Street by the L train.

Warning: Don't take an express train unless you're absolutely sure it stops where you want to go. If possible, pick up a transit map – they're available at some (not all) token booths and newsstands, as well as from the transit office on the main concourse of Grand Central Terminal, from

Central Park Information

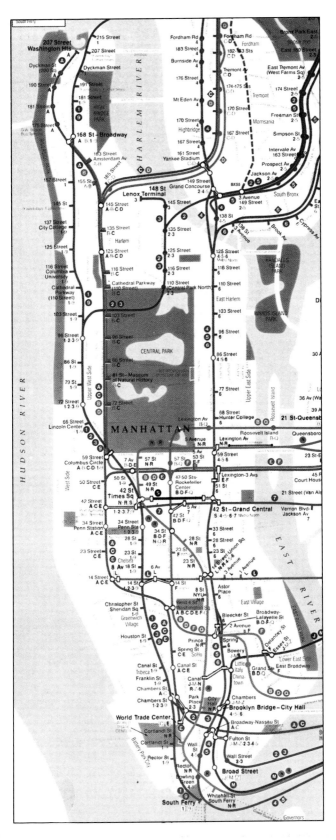

the Visitor Center in Times Square, and from the Convention and Visitors Bureau. Or call the NYC Transit Authority at 718-330-1234.

Subways run 24 hours a day. Service may be limited on some lines after midnight and also on weekends.

Buses

Buses run on most major streets and avenues and cost the same as the subway. You can use a subway token, exact change or the Metro Card, which allows free transfers to the subway as well as another bus. If you're using tokens or change, ask for a transfer, which gets you on your next bus free of charge. In the rush hour it's better walking or taking the subway.

Grab a cab

Taxis

Taxis are convenient but can be expensive. Drivers often don't speak much English and may not know the city well.

If you do take a cab, use the yellow Medallion taxis. These are licensed by the city and insured. Gypsy cabs (independent operators who work without an official license) should be avoided: few have meters, and if you run into any trouble, they are difficult to track down.

Even if you take a cab for only a few blocks, expect to pay at least $5. Tip the cabbie an additional 10 or 15 percent. Cabbies are usually reluctant to break anything larger than a $20 bill, so be sure to ask beforehand if they have change.

By law, taxis are required to take you anywhere in the five boroughs, and to all the airports. The fixed-rate fare to JFK is $30, plus tolls and tip.

Bellboy at the ready

Limousines

Limos can be arranged through most of the best hotels or through limousine services. This is a great way to travel, but only if you've got money to burn.

Driving

Drive in Manhattan only as a last resort. Traffic is heavy, street parking is practically non-existent, and private garages cost an arm and a leg. In short, leave your car at home. The best way to get around Manhattan is on foot. If you need to go long distance, take public transport.

If you need a car to drive outside the city, there are many rental agencies. Check the telephone book for the one nearest your hotel or ask the concierge to help you out. In general, you'll find that national chains have the best selection of cars and the most expensive services. Smaller, local agencies tend to cost less, but their selection and services are limited. In most cases, you must be at least 21 years old to rent a car, and you must have at least one major credit card, although most of the larger agencies require drivers to be 25 years old and have at least two major credit cards.

Always take out liability insurance. Collision insurance is now covered in the rates. Rates are usually at least $65 a day, more depending on the model.

WHERE TO STAY

Hotels

Hotels in Manhattan are expensive. The average room is $162 a night, and in many cases considerably more. However, it is possible to find occasional bargains — and

Washington Square Hotel

even some top hotels offer special weekend rates. The following suggestions are ranked Inexpensive (under $135), Moderate ($150–250), or Expensive (over $250).

Inexpensive

CHELSEA HOTEL
222 W. 23rd St
Tel/Fax: 243-3700
$65 student singles as well as $400 one-bedroom suites available in this bohemian landmark.

HOTEL EXCELSIOR
45 W. 81st St
Tel: 362-9200, Fax: 721-2994
A rambling, circa 1920s hotel close to the Museum of Natural History. Rooms are priced from $109–219.

THE PARAMOUNT HOTEL
235 W. 46th St
Tel: 764-5500, Fax: 354-5237
Stylish, hip and near Times Square. Rooms start at $130 but go way up. The high-tech interiors are by Philip Starck.

PICKWICK ARMS
230 E. 51st St
Tel: 355-0300, Fax:755-5029
Convenient midtown location. Singles start under $85; doubles at $105.

WASHINGTON SQUARE HOTEL
103 Waverly Place
Tel: 777-9515, Fax: 979-8373
Small rooms. Singles at around $95; doubles from $115.

WYNDHAM HOTEL
42 W. 58th St
Tel: 753-3500, Fax: 754-5638
Singles from $120, doubles from $135, and suites from $180. Near Fifth Avenue, West 57th Street and Central Park.

Moderate

THE BARBIZON
140 E. 63rd St
Tel: 838-5700, Fax: 223-3287
Landmark hotel. Smallest rooms start at $190. A great Upper East Side location.

HOTEL BEVERLY
125 E. 50th St
Tel: 753-2700
Small, pretty, and right behind the Waldorf-Astoria. From $160 for singles; $190 for suites. Low weekend rates.

THE FRANKLIN
164 E. 87th St
Tel: 369-1000, Fax: 369-8000
Chic, with a classic video library and complimentary continental breakfast. From $159 single and $179 double. Parking.

GRAMERCY PARK HOTEL
Lexington Ave. at 21st St
Tel: 475-4320, Fax: 505-0535
Quiet and elegant overlooking Gramercy Park. Singles $150; doubles $160; and suites are a true bargain at $180.

THE HELMSLEY MIDDLETOWNE
148 East 48th St
Tel: 755-3000, Fax: 832-0261
Located near the UN. Double rooms start at $165; and suites at under $250. On weekends – presumably when the UN's not in session – it's even cheaper.

HOTEL RADISSON EMPIRE
44 W. 63rd St
Tel: 265-7400, Fax: 315-0349
Near Lincoln Center. Rates $180 and up.

THE SALISBURY HOTEL
123 W. 57th St
Tel: 246-1300, Fax: 977-7752
Close to Carnegie Hall. Rooms include refrigerators, coffee-makers and microwave ovens. From $190 single, $210 double.

SOHO GRAND HOTEL
310 W. Broadway
Tel: 965-3000
Fax: 965-3141
New in 1996, with industrial chic decor, a casually sophisticated restaurant and bar, and a prime Downtown location. Rooms from $249–349, with weekend packages available.

HOTEL WALES
1295 Madison Avenue
Tel: 876-6000
Fax: 860-7000
A small gem located close to Central Park. Rooms from about $189 and standard suites from $269, including breakfast and afternoon tea.

Expensive

THE ALGONQUIN HOTEL
59 W. 44th St
Tel: 840-6800, Fax: 944-1419
Gracious, stuffy and just quirky enough to be interesting. Famed as home to the literary Round Table. Clubby and convenient to the theater district.

Famous name

THE CARLYLE
35 E. 76th St
Tel: 744-1600
Fax: 717-4682
Posh and formal. Includes a very elegant restaurant as well as the Cafe Carlyle, a sophisticated bar/cabaret.

THE DRAKE
440 Park Avenue at 56th St
Tel: 421-0900
Fax: 371-4190
Extremely classic, old world-style hotel, with spacious rooms. The hotel bar is a popular Midtown after-work rendezvous.

HOTEL INTER-CONTINENTAL
111 E. 48th St
Tel: 755-5900, Fax: 644-0079
Classic hotel. Well-equipped health and fitness club exclusively for guests. Moderate weekend packages available.

THE LOWELL
28 E. 63rd St
Tel: 838-1400, Fax: 838-9194
Very elegant and subdued, just off high-powered Madison Avenue.

THE MARK
25 East 77th St
Tel: 744-4300, Fax: 744-2749
Elegant Italian neoclassical suites equipped with kitchenettes. Very service-oriented, with a first-rate restaurant.

THE MILLENIUM HILTON
55 Church St
Tel: 693-2001 or 1-800-HILTONS
One of several new Lower Manhattan hotels, with fabulous views and amenities, but only moderate prices. Weekend specials.

MORGAN'S
237 Madison Avenue
Tel: 686-0300, Fax: 779-8352
Where various discreet glitterati hide out. Doubles are $240 and up, but rates here can also drop on weekends, too.

THE NEW YORK PALACE
455 Madison Avenue and 50th St
Tel: 888-7000
Fax: 303-6000
Exclusive luxury, with formal ambience and decor. Suites come with full kitchens and dining areas.

THE PENINSULA NEW YORK
700 Fifth Avenue at 55th St
Tel: 247-2200, Fax: 903-3949
Art Nouveau furnishings, highly personalized service and superb fitness facilities.

THE PIERRE
2 East 61st St at Fifth Avenue
Tel: 838-8000, Fax: 940-8109
Landmark hotel on Central Park. Rooms are large and elegant; service is top-flight.

THE PLAZA
Fifth Avenue at 59th St
Tel: 759-3000, Fax: 759-3167
The last word in old-world style.

HOTEL PLAZA ATHENEE
37 E. 64th St
Tel: 734-9100, Fax: 772-0958
Very French, very pretty and also very expensive.

REGENCY
540 Park Avenue
Tel: 759-4100, Fax: 826-5674
Ritzy but discreet. This is a favorite with movie-biz people in town to make that big deal.

THE RITZ-CARLTON
112 Central Park South
Tel: 757-1900, Fax: 757-9620
Plush, English-country style and unbeatable views of Central Park. One of the best hotels in New York.

THE ROYALTON
44 W. 44th St
Tel: 869-4400, Fax: 869-8965
Across the street from the Algonquin, but light years away in atmosphere. Ultrachic, some say coldly futuristic. Superb service, and a lobby restaurant frequented by literary types.

WALDORF-ASTORIA
301 Park Avenue
Tel: 355-3000, Fax: 872-7272
Art Deco elegance at its best. Luxurious and centrally located in Midtown.

Suite Hotels

MANHATTAN EAST SUITE HOTELS
Tel: 465-3600; 1-800-ME-SUITE
A group of nine elegant all-suite hotels in the East Side/Midtown area. The concept is akin to renting an apartment, albeit with maid service and hotel amenities. Prices average $155–245 for studio suites; $190–385 for one-bedroom suites; and $380–630 for two-bedroom suites, but special deals are available. Among the best properties are the **Beekman Tower** (First Avenue at 49th St) and the **Surrey Hotel** (20 E. 76th St).

OFF-SOHO SUITES
11 Rivington St
Tel: 353-0860; Fax: 979-9801
Attracts a casually hip clientele; rates start at $97.

Bed and Breakfasts

Single rooms, studios, one- and two-bedroom apartments can be rented through bed and breakfast agencies. Most require a two-day stay and a deposit. Make reservations at least two weeks to a month ahead of time, more if possible. Contact: **City Lights Bed & Breakfast**, Box 20355, Cherokee Station, New York, NY 10028, tel: 737-7049; **Urban Ventures**, 38 W. 32nd St., Suite 1412, New York, NY 10001, tel: 594-5650; **New World Bed & Breakfast**, 150 Fifth Avenue Suite 711, New York, NY 10011, tel: 675-5600

Budget Accommodations

NEW YORK INTERNATIONAL/AMERICAN YOUTH HOSTEL
891 Amsterdam Avenue at W. 103rd St
Tel: 932-2300
Cafeteria, self-service laundry and kitchen available. About $20 a night, plus a membership fee of a few dollars.

YMCA-VANDERBILT
224 E. 47th St
Tel: 756-9600
Some rooms with semi-private baths available; singles start at $57, doubles at $65.

YMCA-WEST SIDE
5 W. 63rd St
Tel: 787-4400
Good value. Access to swimming pool, running track, etc. Rates: $45–65 for singles and $55–75 for doubles.

CALENDAR OF EVENTS

January: The National Boat Show, Jacob Javits Convention Center.
February: The Westminster Kennel Club Dog Show, Madison Square Garden.
Early March: International Cat Show, Madison Square Garden.
March 17: St Patrick's Day Parade, Fifth Avenue.
March: International Art Expo, Jacob Jav

its Convention Center.

Early April: Flower and Garden Show, Rockefeller Center.

April: Ringling Brothers' Barnum & Bailey Circus, Madison Square Garden.

Mid-May: Ukrainian Festival. 7th Street between Second and Third avenues.

Mid-May: Ninth Avenue International Food Festival.

Third Sunday in May: Martin Luther King, Jr Parade, Fifth Avenue.

June: Puerto Rican Day Parade, Fifth Avenue.

Late June: Gay Pride Day Parade, Fifth Avenue.

July-August: Free Shakespeare in the Park, Central Park.

July 4: Macy's Fireworks over the East River.

August: Summer Seaport Festival.

September: Feast of San Gennaro, Little Italy (10 days around the 19th).

October: Hispanic Day Parade, Fifth Avenue.

October: Columbus Day Parade.

October 31: Halloween Parade, Greenwich Village.

Early November: The New York City Marathon.

November 11: Veterans' Day Parade, Fifth Avenue.

Last Thursday in November: Macy's Thanksgiving Day Parade.

December 31: New Year's Eve celebration in Times Square.

BUSINESS HOURS AND HOLIDAYS

Offices: Monday to Friday 9am–5pm.

Banks: Monday to Friday 9am–3pm (larger branches have extended hours as well as Saturday morning hours).

Department stores: Monday to Saturday 10am–6pm, late night Thursday.

Post offices: 10am–5pm. Main branches have Saturday hours.

Celebrating July the 4th

Bear in mind that on the following holidays post offices, banks, government offices and some shops and restaurants close: **January 1** (New Year's Day) ; **January 15** (Martin Luther King Jr's Birthday); **Easter Sunday**; **Last Monday in May** (Memorial Day); **July 4** (Independence Day); **First Monday in September** (Labor Day); **Second Monday in October** (Columbus Day); **November 11** (Veteran's Day); **Last Thursday in November** (Thanksgiving); **December 25** (Christmas)

HEALTH AND EMERGENCIES

For police, ambulance or fire call 911 for immediate help. If you fall ill while staying at a hotel, ask the concierge to summon a doctor or find one yourself in the *Yellow Pages* (under *Physicians* or *Clinics*). If you need emergency medical treatment you can go directly to the nearest hospital. For dental emergencies, call the First District Dental Society for referrals, tel: 679-3966 or 679-4172 after 8pm.

Hospitals

There are at least 20 hospitals in Manhattan. Here are a few of the major ones:

Bellevue Hospital, 462 First Ave, at E. 27th St, tel: 562-4141.

Beth Israel Medical Center, First Ave and 16th St, tel: 420-2000.

Columbia-Presbyterian Medical Center, 622 W. 168th St, tel: 305-2500.

Mount Sinai Hospital, Fifth Avenue and 100th St, tel: 241-6500.

New York Hospital, 525 E. 68th S, tel: 746-5454.

New York University Medical Center, 550 First Ave, tel: 263-7300.

St Luke's-Roosevelt Hospital, Amsterdam Ave at 114th St, tel: 523-4000.

St Vincent's Hospital, Seventh Ave at W. 11th St, tel: 604-7000.

Insurance

Although hospitals are obliged to treat anyone who comes to their emergency rooms, it is essential that you have health insurance. Many private practitioners expect up-front payment for services. If you are unable to pay, and don't have any insurance, you may be turned away.

COMMUNICATION MEDIA

Telephone

New York City is divided into two area codes. **Manhattan** uses 212, **the Bronx, Staten Island, Brooklyn** and **Queens** use 718. The area code in north Jersey is 201, in mid-Jersey 908, in south Jersey 609, on Long Island 516; in Connecticut 203 or 860. To make a long-distance call dial 1 + area code + local number. If you are calling someone within your area code, the prefix is unnecessary.

To dial other countries (Canada follows the US system), first dial the international access code **011**, then the country code: **Australia** (61); **France** (33); **Germany** (49); **Italy** (39); **Japan** (81); **Mexico** (52); **Netherlands** (31); **New Zealand** (64); **Spain** (34); **United Kingdom** (44). If using a US phone credit card, dial the company's access number, then 01, then the country code.

Postal Service and Telegrams

If you don't know where you'll be staying in Manhattan, you can have your mail delivered to you care of General Delivery, at any main post office. You have to pick up General Delivery mail in person and show two pieces of identification.

Because US mail is slow within Manhattan, the use of private bicycle couriers for business correspondence too bulky to fax or e-mail is common. Check the *Yellow Pages* for listings.

Western Union will take telegram messages by phone. Call toll-free for office locations, 1-800-325-6000.

Newspapers and Magazines

The three major newspapers are the *New York Times*, the *Daily News* and the *New York Post*. For listings of events, club dates, gallery shows, etc, check the Friday *Times* 'Weekend' section, and the Sunday *Times*.

Free local papers include the weekly *Village Voice* and the *New York Press*, also great for listings. Magazines worth looking out for include *The New Yorker*, *Time Out New York* and *New York Magazine*, all of which carry excellent listings sections.

A souvenir of your trip

Television and Radio

There are seven televisions stations on the VHF band (2, 4, 5, 7, 9, 11 and 13); several others that broadcast in Spanish and other languages on UHF; and dozens more available on cable, including CNN, TNT and HBO (Home Box Office). Radio in New York is almost as varied. On the FM band, a few of the most popular are WQXR-FM 96.3 (classical), WNEW-FM 102.7 (rock), and WBGO-FM 88.3 (jazz); on the AM band, WOR-AM 710 (talk radio) and WINS-AM 1010 (24-hour news).

FURTHER READING

Non-fiction

Insight Guide: New York City, Apa Publications. A comprehensive look at the city, lavishly illustrated, from the same team that produced this book.

Kinkead, Gwen. *Chinatown: A Portrait of a Closed Society*. Harper Collins, 1992. An in-depth study of one of New York's most fascinating neighborhoods.

Riis, Jacob. *How the Other Half Lives*. Dover, 1971. Groundbreaking photo-documentary on the tenements and sweat shops of the late 19th century.

Sante, Luc. *Low Life*. Vintage Books, 1992. The lures and snares of old New York, from opium dens to street gangs.

Stern, Zelda. *The Complete Guide to Ethnic New York*. St. Martin's Press, 1980. No ethnic stones left unturned.

Symmers, Divya. *Country Days in New York City*. Country Roads Press, 1993. A small but useful guide to the city's less-urban spaces and attractions.

White, N. and Willensky, E. *AIA Guide to New York*. Harcourt, Brace, Jovanvitch, 1988. This is the architecture-lover's bible.

Index

T, U, V

W, Y, Z

Photography	Tony Perrottet *and*
Cover	Manfred Gottschalk
17, 22, 23t, 24t, 25, 27b, 32t, 33, 36,	Bill Wassman
38b, 40b, 41, 46b, 52b, 54, 58, 69,	
73, 79,84, 86	
8/9	Bodo Bondzio
2/3	Catherine Karnow
56t, 68b	Kelly/Mooney Photography
Handwriting	V. Barl
Cover Design	Klaus Geisler
Cartography	Berndtson & Berndtson